Thanks for reading
my book!

Best,

Steve De___

Author's Note

I didn't have a long-term plan to write a book about lizards. I'm not a biologist or reptile fanatic or anything like that. Until recently, I never even had a reptile pet, and even then it was just temporarily so that I could observe and photograph anoles.

Basically, it was just a case of a curious person with a tennis-related injury, on crutches, with some newfound time on his hands. A guy who enjoyed working around the house, in the yard, watching the birds, squirrels, and, of course, the lizards.

In the summer, the lizards can be so thick around homes in Florida you have to be alert and nimble to avoid trampling them on the sidewalk on your way to the front door.

I wondered if the same ones lived in the same spot all the time. Why were most brown, but some black with a back crest, or pale gray? And, occasionally, I would see the lime-green ones; they were always my favorite.

As I began to ask around, I found that few folks even knew the name of these lizards. I thought it kind of disrespectful that we had this unrecognized wildlife. So, I began to ask questions of experts. Their enthusiasm was contagious, and, as I kept digging, I found how many interesting things there were to learn about anoles. Later, I realized this story could have a deeper purpose than just creating an awareness, understanding, and appreciation—perhaps to help preserve our native Florida anoles for posterity.

Suddenly, seemingly distant topics I had often read or heard about seemed up-front and close. Animals losing their habitat due to hyper-development; invader species of plants or animals crowding out those that belonged here; home and business owners caught in a cycle of harmful lawn worship involving mega-doses of water, fertilizer, and pesticides at the expense of native plants that provide habitat for wildlife.

So, here it is. What I learned, and what you are about to learn. —*Steve Isham*

Anoles:
Those Florida Yard Lizards

By Steven B. Isham

Commahawk Publishing LLC
Orlando, Florida USA
www.anolebook.com

Publisher
Commahawk Publishing, LLC
PO Box 547873
Orlando, FL 32854-7873
www.anolebook.com

Publisher Cataloging-in-Publication Data
Isham, Steven B.
Anoles: those Florida yard lizards / Steven B. Isham; illustrations by Henry Flores.
p. cm.
Includes bibliographical references and index.
ISBN-13: 978-0-9789778-4-9 (pbk.)
ISBN-10: 0-9789778-4-x
1. Anoles—Florida. 2. Green anole.
3. Brown anole. 4. Anoles as pets.
I. Flores, Henry, ill. II. Title
QL666.L268184 2006   598.112—dc22

Concept, writing, and page layout by Steven B. Isham, www.anolebook.com
Cover art and all illustrations by Henry Flores,
www.henryfloresgraphics.com
Printed by Color House Graphics, www.colorhousegraphics.com

Contents

The Unlikely Conversation

I saw them in the back yard and they appeared to be arguing. I knew this was not possible, for lizards don't talk. But I had been studying their activities for some time and—real or imagined—these creatures spoke to me in ways that books alone could not.

One was brilliant green, like the first leaves of spring. This slim lizard crawled to the top of a cedar planter not an arm's length away from my recliner.

The second was a yellow-speckled brown—a third larger than the green lizard and with a blunt snout.

The green spoke first: "Hi, my name is Ann and this is Noel. If you say our names fast, one after the other, you'll be stating what we actually are." The voice was high-pitched and feminine, and there was a hint of Southern drawl.

"Come on, try it," she said.

"Ann-noel," I said, a little clumsily. I felt foolish talking to a lizard.

"Again ... faster," she urged.

"An-nole."

"Once more, even faster!"

"A-nole."

"You've said it!" she responded triumphantly. We are anoles (pronounced uh-NOHLS) ... your Florida Yard Lizards."

Our incredible first encounter. Ann
was on the leaf, Noel on the planter.
They called me "Humie," short
for human.

They scampered closer toward me. This was not the behavior of the shy creatures I had observed in Florida over three decades. Scurrying to avoid a human? Yes. But intentionally approaching one? No.

Ann spoke again. She explained that yes, anoles, are on the shy side and, of course, don't talk, but that she and Noel were exceptions. "Like trained chimps for a space mission, we have been specially groomed for another type of event— to educate an uninformed Florida public about who and what we are."

"Well, many people say you are chameleons," I replied.

This time it was Noel, the brown one, speaking. "*Sí, pero este es un gran error...*"

"Not in Spanish, Noel. Excuse him, please; he's originally from Cuba." Then she turned toward Noel and said politely but firmly, "Noel, our communication will be only in English."

"But, me, I express myself so much better in my native tongue," Noel pleaded.

"English, Noel."

"*Ay, caramba!*"

Disappointed but not defeated, Noel continued, "This is exactly why we contact you. We are not the chameleons or other lizards they call us. We are, forever and always, anoles." The voice was raspy and deep for a small lizard. He was very expressive with head and body movements—clearly an excitable sort. "Humans, they see us every day, yet they do not even know our rightful name," he grumbled.

"Yes," agreed Ann, bounding to a young sago palm. "Animal-lovers and the reptile-phobic alike, those who are amused by our antics and those who classify us as pests, they all must know and respect us for what we are—anoles.

"So, we will offer you knowledge, and you will be our messenger," said Ann. "We have five days to complete our task."

Day 1. Hey, We're Not Chameleons!

Noel leaped onto the armrest of my lawn chair. Ann climbed onto a colorful ceramic pot, then stood on a large, glossy schefflera leaf. She began the first lesson by emphasizing that anoles are mistakenly referred to by assorted names, including geckos, salamanders, skinks, and especially "those blasted chameleons."

Noel came closer toward me. He had heard much about chameleons from ancestors' accounts and was eager to contribute.

"Anoles, we are in one sense flattered to be compared to the true chameleon. That is because the chameleon is the 'peacock of lizards.' It is a fact we anoles can change colors but not nearly so impressively as the chameleons."

Ann gave more distinctions. She said true chameleons are Old World lizards— they originate from places like Africa and Asia. As a rule, they do not live in the Western Hemisphere, other than as household pets or escapees.

Chameleons differ from anoles in many physical respects, too, she added. They have mitten-like feet. They have a tongue that can be propelled twice the length of their entire body. They have huge eye enclosures and a strong tail that can be used as an extra leg to grasp branches.

Noel wrapped his own lean tail around a twig on a potted plant. He then attempted to support himself using only the tail but—thump—tumbled to the earth. He, Ann and I had a good belly-laugh over the theatrics. I was pleased that my education would have its lighthearted moments.

"Humie," Noel turned to me. "I can call you Humie?" He pronounced it as if to say *you-me*. "This, it is my friendly way to refer to you as a special HUMAN being. You are special because you are our *estudiante*, or student."

"Humie? Sure, if it pleases you. Humie I am," I nodded.

"*Gracias.* You see, the true chameleons, they are slow-moving creatures,"

Noel said, trudging along as if knee-deep in mud. "But we anoles are quick and nimble."

"Well, how do I know the creatures you call anoles are not geckos?" I said.

Ann replied, "Most geckos love the night life—they are *nocturnal* creatures—and have globe-like eyeballs for night vision. Anoles, on the other hand, are at rest while geckos work and play."

Ann said anoles are *diurnal*, meaning they are daytime lizards. She then repeated the word, pronouncing it slowly, and spelled it phonetically—dI-ur-nul. She promised to break down all difficult words to enhance my pronunciation and learning.

"Geckos are also the most talkative of lizards," Ann continued.

I mentioned that Ann was the chattiest reptile I had ever met.

"I'm referring to the average anole—not to the gifted," she responded. "Ordinary anoles, and most lizards in fact, don't make a peep, but geckos actually

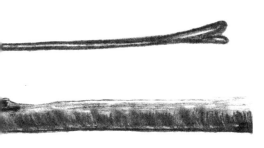

◄ True chameleons don't look anything like anoles. They have feet shaped like mittens for grasping branches, a strong tail that can be used as an extra leg, a harpoon-like tongue, and large, bulging eyes.

bark, grunt, and squeak to communicate with one another."

Noel said he was miffed that chameleons and geckos both had endorsement arrangements with large companies but anoles had no major deals yet. He said two chameleons helped sell a certain adult beverage, and that a gecko was linked with an insurance company.

"Well, how about skinks—maybe you're skinks," I teased.

No, anoles aren't skinks either, Ann stressed. Skinks are most common in Australia and Southeast Asia, although some species are native to Florida. Most skinks have shiny scales that are smooth, as if they had been polished. Their heads tend to be small compared with the long body and tail, and their necks very thick.

"Hmm," I said, "some folks say you're salamanders." Both anoles seemed offended by this comment.

Ann lectured, "Salamanders are not even lizards. They have moist, smooth

Geckos don't resemble anoles or even behave like them. Most are active at night, grunt to communicate, and climb upside-down masterfully.

skin and are actually, ugh, amphibians, like toads." With the mention of amphibians, Ann abruptly swung her nose upward.

She suggested I take a herpetology class, after, of course, I completed anole school. Herpetology, Ann explained, is the study of reptiles and amphibians. She said most herpetologists graduate from a university with a degree in biological sciences. Many are employed by museums, zoos, research laboratories, as park naturalists, and as educators and scientists. She implied that I had a lot to learn, and I had to concede that she was correct.

Skinks have small heads, thick necks and smooth scales that look like they've been polished. Yet many people mistakenly refer to anoles as skinks.

The Origin of Anoles: Just How Old Are They?

Ann said to get comfortable for the continuation of our first day of class. I poured an iced tea and returned to the lawn chair. Noel and I had begun to call Ann "Professor" (good-naturedly, of course) for she was professional, thorough, well-prepared and detailed.

Ann climbed onto a colorful croton plant and chose a branch near my eye-level. Noel remained on my armrest. The shade from a winged elm tree on a balmy day made an ideal setting.

"Anoles are reptiles," she began. "What makes them reptiles?" Ann presented these six traits:

- Reptiles have dry, scaly skin.
- Reptiles breathe with lungs.
- Reptiles have a bony skeleton with strong, flexible backbone and therefore are classified as *vertebrates* (ver-teh-brets).
- Most reptiles (except for snakes) have claws on their feet.
- The great majority of reptiles lay shelled eggs on land.
- Reptiles rely on external sources to help control body temperature.

She went on, "Lizards are just one type of reptile and are generally, though not always, distinguished by having four legs, eyelids that blink (unlike snakes), and ear openings for sound. Other types of reptiles include alligators, crocodiles, snakes and turtles."

Noel was a hoot. Each time Ann introduced a subject, he would support the discussion with exaggerated gestures. When she mentioned dry, scaly skin, Noel jumped off the chair and rubbed his back against the tree bark. When Ann brought up breathing, he began to hyperventilate like an excited baboon. I think he did this partially to enhance my learning, and partially because he was a class clown.

Anole fossils aren't easy to find because small animals don't fossilize well. But some found in the Caribbean are estimated to be 6 million years old.

"Many people confuse reptiles and amphibians," Ann resumed. "But we reptiles are insulted by these mistaken references because we consider ourselves a higher form of life than amphibians."

"Noel," Ann instructed, "name some major differences between reptiles and amphibians." Noel was quick to respond.

"*Sí, Profesora.* Oops, English only. Amphibians, they don't have the claws. Uh, they have a wet, smooth skin—some call it creepy, gooey!" He cackled mischievously, "Ha-ha, aieee! Most lay the eggs in a mess of jello in water. Usually, they begin life in water with no legs, and most use gills to get oxygen from water. Later, they grow the legs and lungs and can live on land but usually stay near shade and water. Either way, young or old, in the water or out, they are slimy and disgusting to me. "Ha-ha, aieee!" he wailed again with what proved to be his signature laugh.

Ann thanked Noel but corrected him that he should have said "jelly-like mass" instead of "mess of jello."

The Professor said scientists believe that reptiles evolved from amphibian ancestors and were the first animals able to live entirely on land. Before reptiles, it was necessary for all vertebrates to live at least a part of their lives in water.

I sipped my tea and reflected on what the Professor had said. I told her I recalled some of this material from my college biology courses, but to please refresh my memory: "When did all this occur? How many eons ago?"

"Fossil records show that some lizards date back to the Jurassic period, some 130 million years ago," Ann informed. "Reptiles were the dominant group of living creatures on earth back then, and they roamed for millions of years. The dinosaurs, well, they perished long ago, but the lizards live on."

"Are anoles descendants of the dinosaurs?" I asked. "I mean, they do look similar in some respects."

"Anoles definitely were not around during dinosaur times," Ann stated. "Anoles do have some distant ancestors that go back to the very end of the dinosaur period—the Mesozoic era—but they are not closely related."

Ann explained that part of the problem in knowing exactly when anoles first appeared is that small lizards do not fossilize well. However, she said there are instances when anoles were trapped in amber sap or fell into sinkholes and were encased in mineral deposits in limestone caves of the Caribbean.

This evidence, she revealed, shows that anoles have been around for about SIX MILLION YEARS!

"Oooh, how creeeeepy," Noel said spookily. He began to walk stiffly, as if mummified.

Professor Ann announced it was time for a 30-minute break, then she and Noel dashed into the garden. I wondered what anoles would do during break.

Where Anoles Fit In With Other Animals

When I returned, Ann was basking in a streak of sunlight on the pine deck. Noel sprinted like a grade-schooler at recess—down the walkway, up the deck steps, over the pottery and onto his familiar armchair position.

"I am pleased to see you're on time," said the Professor. "We have a bit of complex material to cover, so let's pay close attention. Our subject is this: Where do anoles fit in the world of animals in general and other lizards in particular?"

The Professor went on to explain that scientists have created a system called *taxonomy* (tax-ahn-oh-mee) to help us classify living things—plants and animals. She said this is important to science because there are millions of living things in the world—over 2,000 species of lizards alone! Taxonomy uses Latin and Greek names to organize these things into groups with similar features.

She then outlined the major taxonomy classifications for anoles. She pointed out that they start out very general but then become quite specific:

• Anoles are in the Kingdom called *Animalia* (ani-male-e-uh). Plant life is not included in this category.

• Anoles are in the Phylum *Chordata* (kor-daht-uh). This group includes animals with spinal cords. That eliminates worms, insects, and other spineless creatures.

• Anoles are in the Class *Reptilia* (rep-til-e-uh). These animals are born on land, have lungs, and need outside sources to heat and cool the body. This excludes fish, amphibians, birds and mammals.

• Anoles are in the Order *Squamata* (sqwah-mah-tuh). This category consists of lizards and snakes, but not crocodiles or turtles.

• Anoles are in the Suborder *Lacertillia* (las-er-til-e-yuh). Only lizards are members of this exclusive group.

- Anoles are in the Family *Iguanidae* (i-gwan-i-day). This is the family of the iguana lizards, too.

- Anoles are in the Genus *Anolis* (uh-NOHL-iss). This is actually the most widely distributed genus of lizards in the entire Western Hemisphere. That means there are lots of anoles out there.

- Finally, the most specific classification is called the *Species* (spee-sees). Anoles are members of the ... well, there isn't just one species—in fact, there are over 400 species of anoles, Ann taught. Species differ only on a small genetic level. Members of the same species might have different colors or patterns or vary in size, but they are similar in appearance and habits.

"Noel, tell us, what species are you?" Ann asked.

Noel stood proudly at attention—legs thrust high, head erect. "I am of the species *Anolis sagrei* (sag-ree-eye)," he said. "That is our scientific name. But the average people, they know us as the Cuban brown anole, or just brown anole."

"And I am of the species *Anolis carolinensis* (car-o-lin-en-sis)," Ann followed. "But ordinary folks refer to my species simply as the green anole."

"Where did the word anole come from?" I wanted to know.

Ann said the word anole, so far as is known, came from the West Indian word *anoli* (uh-nohl-ee), meaning lizard.

So, Uh, Why Are You In My Yard?

"So you two are entirely different species of anoles, even though you both live in the same yard?" I asked.

"That's correct," said Ann.

She explained that green anoles settled in Florida long before humans were around. "We are actually natives. In fact, we are the only anoles native to this state. We have lived in what you now call Florida for many thousands, perhaps even millions, of years."

"Well, what about Noel and his species?" I asked. "Weren't they here as well?"

"No, brown anoles like Noel are newcomers to the state—Cuban immigrants whose ancestors arrived here only about 60 years ago," Ann explained.

Noel began to sway his head slowly from side to side and hummed what he said was an old Cuban folk song.

"So, how did your species end up here, Noel?"

"How we came to Florida? We stowed away on banana boats, on cigar ships, on lumber lines. Why we came to Florida? To improve our standard of living, to participate in democracy ... "

"Nooooelll, now you're not being truthful," Ann said firmly. "We must not mislead our future spokesman."

"*Ay, caramba!* Okay, so maybe we got lost and wandered into the boat yards."

Ann elaborated, "There are documented instances where Cuban brown anoles were introduced to six different Florida sea ports in the 1940s. There were also pet traders and owners in the Miami area who just liked brown anoles and wanted to establish a population. So they released them to the wild."

"And the other hundreds of species of anoles you mentioned, where do they live?" I asked.

Ann replied that most anoles are in tropical regions. "There are more than 150 species on the West Indies islands in the Caribbean, another 40 or so species in Mexico, and many others in Central and South America. There are about eight other species of anoles in the state of Florida, and, like Noel, they are non-native. But they are not nearly as populous or as widespread as the native green or Cuban brown anoles," she emphasized.

Noel was making a little commotion. He kind of pointed to his belly with one front foot, then opened his mouth and said in a pained voice, *"Profesora, tengo mucha hambre."*

"Repeat that in English, Noel," Ann demanded.

"Oooh, sorry. I am very hungry. I am getting light-headed, weak." He pretended to faint, laying on his back with legs straight up. But chuckling all the while.

Ann called for a one-hour lunch recess. She gracefully scaled the trunk and disappeared into the broadleaf thicket of the elm tree, while Noel dove recklessly through shallow juniper groundcover and into a well-groomed dwarf holly hedge.

I headed toward the house. The sun was now high and warm and the anole activity had really intensified. On the sidewalk, on the lawn, on the hedges, on my brief walk back, I counted every anole I saw. There were 17; all were brown, like Noel. I wondered: Where were Ann's relatives, the green anoles?

Impact of the Invaders

Ann and Noel looked content as class resumed. I asked, "How was lunch?" Ann said they had found something appetizing and promised to address anole diet in a future lesson.

I mentioned my observation of many brown but no green anoles. Ann said this was a timely question for the current lesson.

"Older Floridians will remember vast numbers of green anoles throughout the state many decades ago," Ann began. "But, now, there are fewer greens than ever before. The destruction of Florida habitat and the pressure from invader species, in particular the Cuban brown anole, have reduced our populations in South and Central Florida. Today, green anoles are more commonly found in the upper third of the state."

"The habitat loss I can understand," I responded. "But I thought that you and Noel, the green and brown anoles, were similar species and that you, well, got along peacefully."

Noel was not only less relaxed than before, he looked downright tense, but said nothing.

"Noel and I have a personal understanding and the same objective—to educate the state about anoles," Ann said. "But the fact is, the brown anole populations are expanding rapidly and the green's are declining."

Ann crawled onto a broken branch that had fallen to the ground. "Let me tell you how life has changed for the green anoles," she reflected.

"A long time ago, life was pristine. No pollution or pesticides or bulldozers. There was peacefulness and tranquility. The bright green coats of *Anolis carolinensis* were as numerous as wild ferns, as prominent as fine emeralds.

"Of course," she continued, "intense land development and building booms largely erased that memory, but native green anoles were somehow able to adapt to the habitat and environmental changes. Then, *they* came. The brown anoles. They disturbed the natural ecosystem. Their aggressive behavior drove the green anoles out of their habitats, higher in the trees."

I glanced at Noel. His expression showed compassion to Ann's plight. He took a deep breath and stepped forward. "There are many powerful forces beyond the control of the brown anole," Noel said softly. "We were transported to areas of the state not by our choosing but by chance."

He hopped onto a plant container with purple-flowering heather. "This is how it happened," he said, "in a pot just like this." He slowly walked around the rim. "The plant nurseries, they are a perfect place for reproduction of brown anoles. During all of the housing construction in the 1970s, thousands of browns—born and unborn—they were transported to different parts of the state in tropical landscape plants. The builders, they purchased these plants from nurseries near Miami and the Florida Keys. Remember, that is where many of us beached on the boats from Cuba.

"So, it was not by our choice that brown anole populations spread, but by events we could not control."

Ann harrumphed and whipped her snout high in disgust. But she soon lowered her head and sighed. Evidently, she felt that arguing was to no avail and, worse, would hurt the anole education program.

I suggested we take a break. Noel looked toward Ann and shouted *"olé!"* when she agreed not only to a recess, but to resume studies the following morning.

Both lizards clambered up to my recliner and then, surprisingly, onto my arm. That was the first physical contact we had had. Ann asked if the session had been too stressful, and I replied that, no, we must honestly discuss all issues to ensure that my education is complete and accurate.

With that, Ann darted up the elm tree and Noel bolted into the dwarf holly hedge, as before. Why did they choose the same locations? Were they shortcuts home or did they actually live there?

Day 2.
Where Do They Live?

The following morning, I had breakfast outdoors. The sunshine leaked through fast-drifting, gray-streaked clouds. A husky cardinal splashed in the metal birdbath.

"Alright, time for action," Ann interrupted.

Noel emerged from a bed of periwinkles with a chant of, "Field trip, field trip!"

"Follow me," Ann instructed. I shadowed her down the walkway to the elm tree. "Most anoles are excellent tree-climbers and are therefore called *arboreal* (ar-bor-ee-ul) species," Ann began. She said the Latin word *arbor* means trees. "Generally, we prefer lower elevations, although some green anoles have been seen climbing as high as 100 feet in mature forests."

"So, green anoles actually live in trees?" I asked.

"Well, before the Cuban brown anole arrived in Florida, green anoles didn't have any competitors, so we often lived mainly around the lower trunk of trees. Now we spend more time higher up the tree trunk and into the lower crown."

"Crown?" I asked.

"Yes. That's the area with limbs and branches and leaves. Even today, in areas where there are no brown anoles, you will see greens in the lower parts of trees, with occasional walks on the ground. That's why we are called a *trunk-crown* species."

Ann then outlined a typical home range for green anoles. She began three feet above the lower tree trunk, raced up the tree to the first cluster of branches, then sprinted left and right.

"A male green anole likes a home about this size," she said. "Think of a space 12 feet long x 12 feet wide x 12 feet high, or about 1700 cubic feet. Roughly the size

Green anoles need fairly large living spaces on upper trunks and leafy areas of trees and tall shrubs.

Brown anoles live in small areas on the ground, low-lying shrubs and lower tree trunks.

of a small office. (Ann also converted these numbers into metric measurements—about 3.6 x 3.6 x 3.6 meters, or 48 cubic meters. She said that metrics would be more meaningful to the many international visitors to Florida, the Sunshine State.)

"Females, however, require less space. They live in a small area inside the male's territory. A female green anole needs a space only about 6½ x 6½ x 6½ feet (2 x 2 x 2 meters), or about 280 cubic feet (8 cubic meters)."

"So, you anoles go to the same home every day? You aren't nomads?"

"Basically, as long as our needs are met in one area, there is no reason to move to another. What would cause us to move?" Ann pondered. "One thing is destruction of our habitat. Green anoles prefer tall native grasses, high shrubs, vines, and trees that were once abundant in Florida. Where these native Florida plants are replaced by turf grass and low-growing ornamental plants, green anole activity often declines or disappears."

Looking at the yard, I could understand now at least one reason there were so few green anoles. Not much in the way of tall shrubs or trees. Mostly lots of short non-native plants from the local nursery. And plenty of grass.

"Well, how about Noel, where does he live? ... Where is Noel anyway?" Absorbed by Ann's demonstration, I had lost track of the brown guy.

I heard a rustling noise in the hedge. "Psst, over here," we heard Noel call, but could not see him. Then, I stooped down and spotted Noel under his favorite holly hedge, camouflaged among fallen leaves.

"Ha-ha, aieee! When still, I am practically invisible to the human eye," Noel boasted. "Welcome to my home!"

"This is it?"

"Yes, brown anoles, we are called *trunk-ground* species," Noel said. "We prefer low, thick cover, like a big hedge or plant-covered tree trunk, but we also spend much time on the ground. You will find us in woods and swamps, though we are most at home in areas disturbed by humans."

Ann added, "Brown anoles don't require as much space as green anoles. Remember we said that a green anole male needs a home the size of an average office. But a brown anole male needs only an area about the size of a large office *desk*. Females, again, live in a smaller area inside the male's territory."

"So, Noel and the Cuban brown anoles live mostly on the ground, low shrubs, and lower tree trunks. And Ann and the green anoles live mainly higher on the tree trunk and in the lower leafy area," I summarized.

"*Exacto*," said Noel, "but don't forget that brown anoles can also climb the trees if we have to."

"And that doesn't mean you will never find a green anole on the ground," said Ann, "even though we spend most of our time above it."

Ann said it was time for a well-earned breather. Noel sang a little ditty called "*Tiempo Para un Descanso*," which he translated as "Break Time."

I noticed the temperature had cooled a few degrees as the sun ducked behind cloud cover. Ann and Noel huddled in the path of a sunbeam on a landscape timber. Ann asked that I bring maps to the next session.

Geography, Population & Who's Number 1?

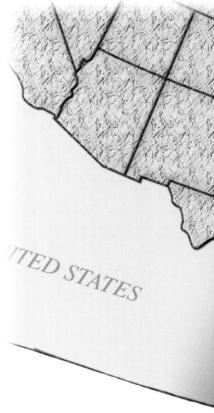

Fifteen minutes later, we were ready to start class again. Ann thanked me for bringing a map book and directed us toward a reclining lawn chair.

"Open to the Americas, please," she said. The hardcover atlas was large and colorful. I put it on my lap and found the map she wanted. Ann startled me by plopping onto the right-hand page. Noel followed close behind. Ann retraced the brown anoles' travels from Cuba to south Florida, and showed the vast areas where anoles live in South America, Central America, and the Caribbean. She reached Florida, then relaxed, her tail laying across the state.

"In the United States, green anoles are most abundant in Florida, but now I am going to show you where else we have gone." She walked in spurts, pausing at several locations. "Green anoles are found in every Southeastern state, including portions of North Carolina and Tennessee." She then headed westward, stopping in Texas and Oklahoma. "We are here, too."

I was impressed. "Green anoles can survive in cold temperatures like those in Tennessee?"

"It is not easy, and all certainly do not endure the severe winters, but some green anoles have evolved to withstand these colder conditions," Ann replied. "Remember that greens are the only anoles *native* to lands north of Mexico. So, some have been able to adapt from their usual *subtropical* weather—as in Florida— to the cooler, temperate climates further north. But they can survive only in small,

Ann outlined the states where green anoles are found today. But she worried about their future in Florida because of the brown invaders.

sunny microhabitats that face the south."

Ann said that other anole species, Noel's included, are originally from very warm *tropical* climates, like Cuba's, but have now made the transition to cooler, sub-tropical climates, like Florida's. Even so, they cannot survive in the colder temperate regions. "The furthest north that the Cuban brown anoles have gone so far is southern Georgia, Louisiana and Texas," she said.

"And we are in the other place, too, the paradise!" Noel squealed.

"Yes, Noel, thanks for the reminder. Brown and green anoles both have found their way to Hawaii," Ann revealed.

Noel wished he could visit Hawaii someday because he suspected the female anoles had learned to hula. He swiveled his lower abdomen and tail in a slow rhythm.

Meanwhile, Ann proceeded with a population lesson.

"How many anoles are there in the state of Florida? The number is so great that no authority will even guess." Noel thought it might be a "gazillion trillion" but Ann said that could not be confirmed. Scientists have found, however, that there can be up to about 4,000 Cuban brown anoles per acre (10,000 per hectare)!

"What we do know is this," Ann stated. "In both natural settings and scientific test sites, green anole populations fall sharply when brown anoles are introduced."

I asked how this could be proven.

"These tests are done on tiny remote islands dredged up in the ocean, so that no lizards can enter from outside territories," Ann said. "In one study, a scientist counted 125 green anoles on a little dredge island one year. Then he came back a year later and counted only 12. Meanwhile, the brown anole population increased from 18 to more than 300."

Why does this occur? Ann explained that brown anoles are very aggressive, stockier, breed faster, and live more densely. In fact, the brown anole is clearly the most abundant vertebrate walking the ground in the entire state.

"To put it even more dramatically," Ann said, "there are those who now say that the Cuban brown anole has become the widest-ranging reptile anywhere on earth."

"And word is out that the brown anole has recently been seen in Asia, in Taiwan." Ann divulged.

"We're number one!" Noel chanted while high-stepping like the drum major of a marching band.

Territoriality &
Body Language

Noel became very lively as Ann announced that territoriality would be the subject of the next lesson.

"This is where they are separated, the true macho males from the cowards," Noel strutted.

Ann encouraged him to lead the session.

Noel began, "No matter what the color—green or brown—anole males must find, claim and defend their territory, especially during the mating season. Sometimes, a male, he will roam an area as long and far as a football field to find a territory. Then, once he claims it, he becomes like a soldier guarding the fort."

Back and forth Noel stomped. He said, "This territory, it must provide shelter from weather and enemies, it must have food and water resources, and," smiling slyly, "it must be suitable for as many *señoritas*, the females, as the male can maintain and protect."

"Whew," I said, "so you're competing against other males for a territory?"

"This is the essence of the male anole life—the ultimate conquest," Noel said spiritedly. "Males without a territory, they are possibly without mating companions and doomed endlessly to challenge for their own real estate."

"It sounds like combat," I said.

"During the mating season, yes, it can be combat," Noel said. "Look, here in my shrub, I will show you what happens when another male tries to invade my territory." Noel hopped down to the ground. "*Profesora*, you will play the part of the intruder," he insisted.

Ann agreed and pretended to encroach on Noel's shrub. Noel straightened his front legs and began to bob his head up and down. Then he dropped a big reddish-orange flap from beneath his throat.

Noel began to bob his head up and down. Then he straightened his front legs and did push-ups. ...

"That is magnificent, Noel!" I said. "I have seen anoles do that many times in my yard."

"Yes, this is what we call *displaying*," Noel related. "This is one way we try to frighten the aggressor."

"What if it doesn't work?"

"Then I start with the push-ups," Noel said, "Watch this." He used his legs like pistons to lift himself up and down several times. "It is intimidating, no?"

"Very much so, but what if the aggressor still doesn't leave?"

Noel was outraged. He yelled, "It is my territory and shall not be taken!" and began to change physical appearance. "Watch the color," he commanded. And then he turned from light brown to black. "The color change, it shows that I am angry," he growled. Suddenly a crest appeared on the neck and back. It made Noel appear much larger than before.

"Noel, you are really a warrior now!" And I was sincere, too. With the head-bobbing, push-ups, radiant throat fan, jet-black body, and protruding crest, Noel was transformed from an ordinary male anole into a gladiator. "If I were an invader, I would definitely turn tail and head the other way," I said.

"You would unless you were equal in size, or bigger or stronger. Or maybe stupid. If this happens, we both puff up our bodies, and our tails may wag as we try to make the other back down. We will parade around each other for many minutes until one, he cowers and slips away."

"But what if both refuse to back down? Then what?"

"Then there is no alternative but to fight," Noel said resolutely.

"This is where the actress exits the stage," Ann laughed as she headed to a nearby sun-soaked spot. "Anoles have social rules, too. Females and males generally do not fight each other."

I wanted to know more about the throat fan that Noel had displayed. And the crest on the back. And color changes. Ann assured me these subjects would be addressed as we moved onto the topic of anatomy. As she spoke, I noticed that Noel was brown again, and the back crest and throat fan were gone.

"What a change—from Superman to Clark Kent again!" I said.

Ann explained that Noel was actually communicating during his metamorphosis. "Because anoles can't talk, we have to use other methods to communicate. In this case, Noel was expressing anger to protect his territory; but anole males may also use the same displays to impress females."

"*Sí, sí,*" Noel cooed. "The ladies love our displays. It is maybe like a human male flexing the muscles in a tight shirt sleeve."

"Are the push-ups and head movements also a way to communicate?" I asked. Noel and Ann giggled as I clumsily tried to mimic their displays.

"Most definitely," said the Professor. "Each anole species has a unique head-bob that enables other members of the same species to identify it. We communicate with our posture; with our movements as we walk, strut or bob; and with our use of space—for example, seeking greater height to appear taller. As Noel showed us, a tall stance, extended throat fan, and erect dorsal crest can be scary."

Ann then formally defined several major anole displays:

Next he dropped a colorful throat fan and raised a crest along his back.

- **Push-Up:** A raising and lowering of the body by flexing and extending the legs.

- **Head-Bobbing:** Up-and-down head movements that are probably the most expressive part of the anole language. They can be used to greet, bid farewell, brag, warn, attract and repel. Head-bobs are often used with the throat fan extended and can occur one at a time or in bursts called a *volley*.

- **Shudder-Bobbing:** The head appears to vibrate or shake rapidly, followed by the upswing and bouncing of other bobs. Shudder-bobbing is mainly used by males during courtship.

- **Swagger:** The lizard stands on straightened legs and compresses its body to make it look taller. The tail may be slightly arched and swished from side to side.

- **Changing Direction:** When very close to each other, anoles sometimes display while walking in the same direction. It may appear almost as though they are mirror images of the other.

Ann said we were right on schedule and dismissed class for the day. I watched again as they raced toward their territories—Ann scaling the elm and Noel bursting into the bush. Having trimmed and manicured the hedge many times, I could certainly understand why Noel had chosen it as his home. Not only did it provide outstanding cover in the form of thick foliage, it was strong and springy and not easy to penetrate.

Day 3. Anatomy & The Senses

We opened the third day of anole school under clear skies, increasing humidity, and early-morning sunshine. As Ann looked for a good spot to teach amid the purple leaves of a young mock cherry tree, I thought how much she resembled a miniature alligator: scaled skin, long tail, streamlined body, and narrow, triangular, flat head with long jaws. Noel bounded along presently, and I noticed that he had the same general features, but was stockier with a short snout.

The Professor announced that our next subject, anatomy, was somewhat complicated and that we should be alert. The lean, low branch swayed gently with each of her movements and gestures.

"Where shall we start?" asked the Professor. "How about the skin—yes, begin outside and work our way in. Noel, come up here," she said, pointing toward a nearby limb. "You will be the specimen."

"Oh, this, it is such an honor, *Profesora*!" Noel gushed with his natural enthusiasm. "Always I have wanted to be the specimen." He then posed totally still, like a freeze-model.

"Lizards have quite a bit in common with humans," Ann began. "First, we are both vertebrates. That means we have a bony skeleton that provides a support structure for muscles, organs, blood vessels, and other parts, all of which are wrapped up in skin. Like humans, we also have ligaments, tendons, and muscles, providing us with flexibility, agility and strength."

As a point of interest, Ann added that there are some 45,000 species of vertebrates worldwide. Of these, over 8,000 are reptile species.

The Professor noted that lizards, like many other animals, have two layers of skin. The inner layer (dermis) is made of tissues, blood vessels, nerves, and pigments for color change, and is not shed. As in humans, the outer layer of skin,

Noel seized and then swallowed a piece of shedding skin. I learned that the new, looser layer of skin gives anoles room to grow.

called the epidermis, serves as a protective barrier for the deeper tissues. But on lizards, the outermost portion of the epidermis is made of a substance called *keratin* (kair-uh-tin)—a tough, fibrous protein—which thickens and forms the scales we see. Keratin is the same substance found in human hair and nails.

Ann said the scales serve several important functions:

• Scales provide a waterproof barrier, allowing lizards to live away from water without suffering from dehydration.

• Scales offer protection against wear and tear as rough objects are contacted.

• Scales provide a barrier against certain potentially harmful wavelengths of sunlight.

• Variations in scales are also another means of distinguishing one species of lizard from another.

Ann invited me to examine Noel's skin through my 10X handheld magnifying glass. "Note how the scales differ in shape, in size, and in how they are arranged," she said.

The skin was fascinating under magnification. Some scales were smooth, some overlapped like stacked tiles, some lined up neatly against one another, some were like small grains or bumps, some had a ridge down the center—like the keel on the bottom of a boat. The chest and belly were white, with finer scales. But, here, too, the scales were irregular, wonderfully random.

"Anole skin does not grow with the rest of the body," Ann continued. "As the lizard grows, the outer keratin layer is shed. But unlike a snake skin, anole skin does not peel in one large, continuous piece. It sheds in bits and pieces—like a human peeling after a sunburn. We call it *molting* (mol-teeng)."

"Look, Noel's got a piece of skin peeling off his side," I observed. Noel suddenly broke from his trance, lunged left, snatched the peeling skin with his jaws, ripped it away from his body, and swallowed it.

"How repulsive," I thought to myself, whereupon Ann commented, "That is a form of grooming—biting, pulling, and swallowing the shedding skin. Anoles do this for two reasons. One, because it assists in the removal of the skin, which may cause discomfort, irritation and even loss of appetite. You may see anoles rubbing against rocks or other rough surfaces to help removal, too. And, two, because the skin contains valuable nutrients."

"I find it also quite the tasty treat," Noel burped. "Sometimes, we even eat the skin off of other anoles."

"Now that I have trouble *swallowing*—pun intended," I countered.

Ann said the new skin is brighter and looser, giving anoles more room to grow. And because they continue to grow throughout their lives, anoles always need to shed their skin—as many as several times a year.

I looked closely at Noel's skin without magnification. It appeared almost velvety. The black and brown colors were mixed and mottled. I also noticed some V-shaped patterns, kind of like a military sergeant's stripes, on both sides of the ridge down the center of the back. "Are those common?" I asked.

"Good observation," Ann praised. "Anoles can have an endless variety of skin patterns, but many brown anole males, like Noel, have the V-shaped *chevrons* you noticed. The yellow specks on Noel's side are also common. Female brown anoles frequently have vertical stripes or diamond-shaped patterns down the back.

"On the contrary," Ann compared, "green anoles, like me, do not have the many and varied patterns and markings of the brown anoles. The one exception is that green anole females often have a light-colored line down their backs."

A Peek Inside
The Anole

Ann said she needed a volunteer for a brief lesson on internal anatomy. Noel, of course, immediately stepped forward.

"Thank you, again, Noel," Ann said. "This time, we need a specimen to, uh ... dissect."

"Dissect, of course, I am available for any ... wait a minute! This one, I better check the English-Spanish translation. Dissect? Does that not mean to cut, *Profesora*?"

"Yes, Noel," Ann said straight-faced. "We would need to open you up with a surgeon's scalpel to examine your internal parts and then ..."

"No, no, no, *Profesora*! That is not for me," Noel appealed.

"Well, we would stitch you back up, of course. Now see here, Noel. Are you withdrawing your offer? You did volunteer to be the specimen, didn't you?" Ann pressed, tongue-in-cheek.

"Yes, Noel, I heard it, too," I played along.

"But, but, I didn't know you need to cut ... *ay, caramba!* I don't like the sharp things. Me, I am even uneasy around the cactus needles."

"Okay, Noel. I guess we don't really need to operate after all," Ann said. "How about if we just continue our discussion."

"Whew!" Noel exhaled.

Anoles are physiologically similar to mammals and birds in many respects, Ann said. They have nervous, circulatory, and respiratory systems. They have a brain, heart, kidneys, and other familiar organs. She said there unfortunately was not enough time to cover each of these in detail, so she would be selective.

• **Lungs:** Anoles and other reptiles breathe with lungs. And, unlike amphibians, they don't go through a stage where they have gills.

- **Heart:** Do anoles and other lizards sit motionless for long periods because they have an inefficient heart? The old school of thought said "yes." But not today's.

Unlike birds and mammals with their four-chamber heart, lizards have what is considered a primitive three-chamber heart. In birds and mammals, blood containing oxygen is separated from blood without oxygen as it flows through the heart and to the rest of the body. This efficient system helps to support their very active lifestyles.

For many years, it was believed that these two types of blood were mixed together in the lizard heart. The theory was that lizards were less active because the oxygen-containing blood was diluted by oxygen-less blood. However, it is now known that the *pattern* of blood flow ensures that the two streams remain apart, even though the blood is not physically separated in the lizard heart.

In short, lizards are less active than birds and mammals for other reasons. These include a slower energy metabolism and limited amount of oxygen they can take in with their small, simple lungs.

- **Brain:** One of the largest areas of the anole brain is the part associated with vision. That's because they are very visual creatures. The adult brain is about $3/16$ inch (5 millimeters) wide and up to ½ inch (12 millimeters) long. This includes the smell-related parts, which stick out like two stalks in front of the brain.

- **Glands:** Anoles have many glands, like humans do. For example, the thyroid gland helps develop healthy bones by regulating the metabolism of phosphorus and calcium. And the pituitary gland produces hormones that affect growth, reproduction, and other functions. But there are differences, too.

Perhaps most interestingly, anoles have no sweat glands. When humans are hot, sweat glands secrete liquid through pores all over the body as a cooling method. But lizards have pores only in a small area on the underside of the thighs and tail base—and do not sweat. Lizards do, however, have glandular secretions that help the opposite sex of a species recognize one another. Male lizards, in particular, mark their territories by secreting a waxlike substance through their pores.

"Kind of like a dog marking his spot on a fire hydrant, right?" I proposed.

"Yes," said Noel, "except that the male anole, he drags his rear-end like this, over the area he wants to mark." Noel crept slowly and labored, as if he were muscling a heavy chain up a steep hill.

"Incidentally," Ann added, "the fact that lizards don't sweat is another way they maintain fluids, enabling them to survive without spending time in water."

- **Digestive System:** Anoles lubricate (wet) their food with mouth saliva, but major breakdown occurs in the lizard's stomach. The food is further broken down as it moves to the small intestine, where the nutrients are absorbed into the body. After several hours, the contents are passed to the large intestine, where the digested material is dried and prepared for excretion.

When the lizard eliminates waste, uric acid (urine) from the bladder and feces (poop) from the rectum are combined in a cavity called the *cloaca* (kloh-ay-kuh). The mixed wastes are shoved out of the cloaca, through a vent, to the outside of the body. The multipurpose cloaca is also where female lizards mate and release eventual offspring.

Exploring the Mouth, Nostrils & Ears

"Open wide, Noel," Ann prodded.

Noel obeyed, but with a ferocious gnashing and hissing. "Reminds you of T-Rex, no?" Noel said.

"Yes, you definitely resemble a small-scale dinosaur," I said. "I don't see how paleontologists could say otherwise."

"Inside the mouth," Ann began, "we find, as in many animals, teeth and tongue. Notice that anoles have only a small pink blob of a tongue. It is quite muscular and fixed to the jaw."

"So the tongue doesn't stick way out, as in some lizards?" I asked.

"Only the front half protrudes, usually when drinking," Ann replied.

"Anoles differ a lot in this respect from lizard species like chameleons. True chameleons have that long sticky tongue to extend and retract rapidly for food capture. But they are slow-moving lizards and a slingshot tongue is necessary for their survival. Anoles, on the other hand, rely more on their stealth, speed and agility."

"How about some of the lizards I've seen with forked tongues?" I said. "Anoles don't need a forked tongue?"

"I suppose it would be nice to have one," Ann mused, "because lizards with forked tongues often have the most highly developed sense of smell. The monitor lizards, for instance, flick out their forked tongue like snakes do. The tongue picks up tiny particles in the air and transmits them to a special organ, called the Jacobson's organ, at the roof of the mouth, near the nostrils. The organ consists of small pits or sacks and translates information about odors for the brain to process."

Ann said that snakes and monitor lizards have a well-defined Jacobson's organ, but anoles and some other lizards with short, broad tongues do not. Anoles

*Noel opened his mouth to reveal
many dagger-like teeth and a pink tongue.*

may lean down and lick an object briefly for information but they cannot flick the tongue in mid-air and retrieve valuable scents like the forked-tongue lizards can.

So, even though anoles have nostrils and a Jacobson's organ, their sense of smell is poor, Ann concluded.

Noel had kept his mouth open the entire discussion. Ann described it as gaping—a wide, sustained opening of the jaws.

"Isn't he getting tired?" I wondered.

"Heavens, no," Ann said. "We anoles can keep our mouths open for a long time without fatigue. We often open wide to intimidate others or to signal that we are annoyed." She added that, because lizards don't perspire, they also sometimes partially open the mouth just to pant as a way to cool off.

"Now let's inspect the teeth," Ann instructed. "Notice that all of them are the same. We don't have canines, incisors or molars, like many mammals have. Our teeth are shaped like identical little daggers, and can wound other anoles during a fight, piercing the skin and even drawing blood." Ann said that each anole can have up to about 80 teeth.

"Now you know something about our sense of smell and dental work, but how about hearing?" said Ann. "Noel, why don't you take that question?"

Monitor lizards differ from anoles in that they have forked tongues and an excellent sense of smell.

"We anoles have pretty good hearing, especially when we can use it together with a visual—how do you say, uh—sighting," Noel said. "Sometimes we know the enemies, they are coming our way. We can hear them crunching the leaves or pounding the dirt. We pick up even slight vibrations on the ground."

Ann added, "As you have probably noticed, anoles and other reptiles don't have external ears like mammals. Our ear drums aren't inside the head, either. Ours are built right onto the sides of our head, just behind the jaws, see? Each ear drum, called a *tympanum* (tim-pa-num), is made of a thin membrane. We hear sounds as the ear drum vibrates and causes movement of bone, membranes, and fluids inside the inner ear."

Another interesting fact: Ann said you can shine a light in one anole ear and usually see it through the ear on the other side! That's because there are no muscles separating the inside of the throat from the ear, as in mammals. It's just one big cavity.

Ann encouraged me to inspect Noel's ear openings with the magnifying glass. He saw my enlarged face through the magnifier and gave a startled "yaaah"! "Oh, it is just you—a giant Humie," he said, relieved. Then added, "You know, I could use that magnifier to make myself look bigger to my competitors."

"But how would you carry it?" I challenged.

"Hmm..."

Noel said he personally looked forward to the afternoons when the dudes got out of school and drove by with windows open and the radio on. But Ann cautioned that anoles are sensitive to sound vibrations and should not be exposed to loud music.

Precision Vision: What They See

Ann held very still so I could see the turret-like enclosure around her eye, and the ear opening just beyond the mouth.

Up close, Ann's eyes were beautiful. The eyeball was dark and round, and sometimes surrounded by a yellow or turquoise rim. She blinked slowly, and, as she did, the eye closed into a narrow slit. Each blink cycle took about 2 seconds. Ann said that, unlike snakes, anoles and most other lizards have moveable eyelids that open and close in the normal manner, up and down. In addition, there is an inner semi-transparent membrane that slides across the eye to clean off dirt and keep the surface moist.

Ann invited me to examine her eyes more closely from all angles. From behind her head, I could see a round enclosure around each eye. Ann called it a *turret* (tur-it). She said the turret is actually formed by the eyelids, which are slightly fused at the edges. "Anoles have great scope of vision because the eyeball is positioned slightly outside the orbit of the skull and is small compared with the size of the turret," she explained. "Anoles can rotate their eyes around independently—not as spectacularly as a true chameleon but still very nicely."

Noel demonstrated this by rotating each eye in a different direction at the same time. As he did, I slowly, secretly moved my left hand from near the ground up toward his tail.

"So, why you do you try to touch me back there?" he questioned matter-of-factly.

"Wow, you saw me sneaking up."

"Yes, of course, this is what we are trying to tell you. We can see in many directions because our eyeballs, they orbit like the Space Shuttle."

Ann mentioned that outstanding peripheral (side) vision and independent eye movement are two of the ways anoles are able to spot and avoid enemies.

I thought, "How well-equipped you anoles are for vision. You've got eyes that rotate like a tank gunner. But can you see colors, or just black and white?"

"Definitely colors," assured Ann. "In fact, color vision is one of the ways we are able to distinguish one species of anole from another. We can see the color of both the skin and the displaying throat fan."

"And how far away can you see these colors, and other anoles and objects in general?"

"Easily 10, 15, 20, even 30 feet away (up to 10 meters)," Ann said. "We anoles have sharp vision. Territorial males are always flashing long-distance displays at their neighbors."

"And this is why we don't need those things you wear on top of your nose," Noel chuckled.

"On top of my ... oh, of course. My eyeglasses!" I grinned. "Listen, why do you anoles sometimes cock your head and glare with one eye while on other occasions you appear to look straight ahead with two eyes?"

"Excellent question, Humie," Ann lauded. She then explained the differences between these two types of vision.

When anoles use both eyes to focus on a single object, they are said to be using *stereoscopic*, or *binocular*, vision, just like humans and dogs and other sophisticated animals do. They use binocular vision because it gives them *depth perception* and therefore a *distance* estimate.

But anoles have only limited binocular vision. This is because their eyes are on the side of the head, and they are able to focus on only a very narrow overlapping field directly in front of their head. So, once they have used binocular vision to establish perspective, they cock their head to look more carefully out of one eye, and are said to be using *monocular* vision.

Anoles have monocular vision to the sides and rear of the head. In combination with their binocular vision, this gives them almost a 360-degree view. The one place they cannot see is directly behind themselves.

Of further interest, Ann revealed, anoles have something in common with sharp-sighted birds of prey—two retinal *foveae* (fo-vee). Each *fovea* (fo-vee-uh) is a pitted area in the retina of the eye—sort of a narrow tunnel—where vision is very sharp. In fact, anoles are members of the only non-bird group known to have two foveae—one for fine monocular vision and another for binocular vision.

"Fascinating," I said.

Ann said anoles also see light in the ultraviolet range. So, they're seeing vibrant colors, contrast and details not apparent to humans, but very distinct, vivid, and exciting among themselves.

I had taken many notes from our anatomy and related lessons and was a little overwhelmed. For the first time, I was actually grateful when Ann dismissed class for the day. I was so much more learned than just 72 hours ago, I thought. Now I know something about anole history, habits, anatomy. What could be next?

Ann flexed her legs and sprang onto the elm while Noel leaped crazily from one rock to another until he reached the home hedge.

Subscribe & Save

SPECIAL INTRODUCTORY PRICE

☐ **1 YEAR (12 ISSUES) $16.95—SAVE 72% OFF THE COVER PRICE!**

SAVE EVEN MORE ☐ **2 YEARS** (24 issues) $26.95   **BEST DEAL!** ☐ **3 YEARS** (36 issues) $36.95
78% savings!   80% savings!

And receive a FREE GIFT—*Along the Gulfshore 2-for-1 ArtsTicket Book*

NAME _____

ADDRESS _____

CITY _____ STATE _____ ZIP _____

E-MAIL _____ PHONE _____

☐ PLEASE BILL ME   CREDIT CARD # _____

☐ PAYMENT ENCLOSED   ☐ VISA ☐ MC ☐ AMEX   EXP DATE _____

☐ SIGN UP TO RECEIVE *WEEKEND INSIDER*, OUR FREE WEEKLY E-NEWSLETTER

E-MAIL _____ @ _____

Add $20 per year for Canadian subscriptions; add $30 per year for overseas.
For fastest service, call (800) 881-2394 or visit our Web site, www.SarasotaMagazine.com.
SATISFACTION GUARANTEED!

SBD0910

NO POSTAGE
NECESSARY
IF MAILED
IN THE
UNITED STATES

BUSINESS REPLY MAIL

FIRST-CLASS MAIL   PERMIT NO. 69   SARASOTA FL

POSTAGE WILL BE PAID BY ADDRESSEE

CURTCO/GSM LLC
330 S PINEAPPLE AVE STE 205
SARASOTA FL 34236-9698

Jet Lag & Cyclops: A Third Eye

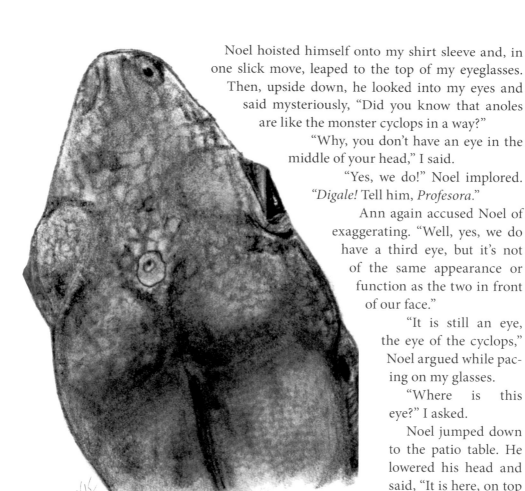

Noel hoisted himself onto my shirt sleeve and, in one slick move, leaped to the top of my eyeglasses. Then, upside down, he looked into my eyes and said mysteriously, "Did you know that anoles are like the monster cyclops in a way?"

"Why, you don't have an eye in the middle of your head," I said.

"Yes, we do!" Noel implored. *"Digale!* Tell him, *Profesora.*"

Ann again accused Noel of exaggerating. "Well, yes, we do have a third eye, but it's not of the same appearance or function as the two in front of our face."

"It is still an eye, the eye of the cyclops," Noel argued while pacing on my glasses.

"Where is this eye?" I asked.

Noel jumped down to the patio table. He lowered his head and said, "It is here, on top of the head."

"Where? I can't see anything."

Ann signaled me to use the hand-magnifier again, explaining, "Noel is showing us what we call the *parietal* (pair-I-eh-tal) eye, also sometimes called the *pineal* (pI-nee-ul) eye. Many reptiles have this third eye. Like a normal eye, it has a cornea, a lens and a retina with photoreceptive cells, but it does not form a visual image."

"No image? You can't really see anything with this eye?" I said as I struggled with the magnifier. "Then what is the purpose?"

"Biorhythms," Ann and Noel said together.

"Biorhythms? You mean like when people travel overseas and have to recover from jet lag?"

"Yes," said Ann, "the third eye is a tool that sets our biological clocks. It records the duration and intensity of daylight at different times of year. The light zaps the pineal gland, just beneath the third eye, and the gland secretes hormones to set our moods, daily activity rhythms, and reproductive schedules according to the season."

"Can you see my cyclops eye yet, Humie?" Noel persisted.

"There it is," Ann pointed out. "It shows up as just one small scale—kind of like frosted glass—in the middle of the head."

"Yes, I see it now," I said.

"Scientific studies have shown that anoles will become less active if you cover up the third eye, even though the two regular eyes still see daylight," Ann added.

"Remarkable," I said.

"Even more remarkable are the five magical physical traits next on our agenda," Ann asserted.

Magic Trait #1: Walking Straight Up

Ann whispered into Noel's right ear. Noel chuckled playfully and sped toward the window. He sprang onto a pane of glass and then began to crawl up the vertical surface.

"It is magic, no?" said Noel as he continued the Spiderman-like stunt. "Did you ever wonder how anoles, we can walk straight up like flies, and on smooth stuff like glass?"

"Of course, I have marveled at your agility many times," I replied, "but, no, I honestly do not know how you succeed. Is there something sticky on the soles of the feet?"

"No, nothing like that," Noel said. "No glue, no goo, no suction cups. The feet are perfectly dry."

"The trick is mother nature's toe-pads with *lamellae* (luh-mel-ee)," Ann explained.

"What in Godzilla's name are lamellae?"

Ann motioned for me to pick up the magnifier again.

We zeroed in on Noel's feet. "Anoles have five toes on each foot. Underneath each toe are the lamellae. As you can see under magnification, they look like flaps with horizontal ridges," said Ann. "But only with a powerful electron microscope can you see that each flap is covered with millions of tiny hair-like projections called *setae* (see-tee). Each hair, or *seta* (see-tuh), is more than 100 times thinner than a human hair."

"Wow, that is hard to imagine!"

"And on top of the setae are triangle-shaped tips called *spatulae* (spa-chu-lee) that latch onto the surfaces we climb," Ann said excitedly. "Just imagine a miniature paint brush full of flexible bristles. The anole crawls up smooth surfaces

Noel clung to the glass effortlessly. With the magnifier,
I could see the toe-pads used to climb smooth surfaces.
The claws are used on tree bark and other objects
where they can get a grip, Ann said.

by dragging its feet and then peeling these adhesive bristles up and away from the surface. This works far better than trying to lift an entire foot at once."

"Kind of like peeling up a piece of tape?" I asked.

"Yes, but everything is held together by molecular force," she said.

"How do you mean?"

"Scientists say that unbalanced electrical charges around molecules in the foot-hairs and climbing surfaces attract each other. That's why anoles have fantastic clinging ability."

Ann then supported her entire weight using only the toes on one foot as she dangled from a tabletop.

"Exceptional cling power!" I said.

Noel was now darting around like a leashless puppy at the park. He raced across a polished tile walkway and then shinnied up a glossy vase. "Our special toes also allow us to run, dodge, and turn quickly—even on slick objects," he demonstrated.

"Awesome, Noel. Can you climb totally upside down, too?"

Noel whisked over to me and confessed, "Not usually. For that you will have to see the geckos. They are the expert ceiling climbers of the lizard world."

"That is a fact," Ann conceded. "Geckos, too, have lamellae, setae, and spatulae. But their gripping power is far beyond that of anoles."

"Now back to our feet," said Ann. She and Noel both extended their right front legs. "You will notice some differences between us. Brown anoles have longer legs because they are built to run on the ground and jump from one shrub to another. But greens have larger toe-pads to help us creep along slender tree branches."

Ann also showed that four toes on each foot are tightly bound together. But the fifth toe, particularly on the rear feet, shoots out at an awkward angle. That's because the bone in this outside toe is shaped like the letter "L."

I got a good look at the claws on their feet, too. Ann said that lamellae are great for smooth surfaces, but the long, flexible claws are handy for climbing trees, rocks, and other surfaces where anoles can get a grip.

"You know, we have already described important differences between anoles and true chameleons, but here is yet another example," the Professor said. "Our feet and theirs are entirely different in looks and function. Chameleons have a much more powerful grip thanks to strong toes arranged in bundles of two on one side and three on the other."

Magic Trait #2:
The Tail That Grows Back

Ann said that lizards are the most advanced form of vertebrates able to regenerate a body part—namely, the tail.

"Is it common for anoles to lose their tails?" I asked.

"Well, it does not happen to every one of us but it has saved the life of many anoles," Noel said.

"I would say at least 10% of adult anoles in the wild lose their tails," Ann ventured.

"And how does that typically happen?"

"Trying to escape!" Noel blurted. "The enemy will grab the tail; he wants to have you for the *bocado*—oh, that is the Spanish word for 'snack'—but the tail it will break and the anole he will run free."

"And there's a word for this event: It's called *autotomy*," Ann said. "I'll repeat it for you and spell it phonetically: aw-tot-oh-mee.

Ann noted that autotomy means "self-amputation." The animal is able to shed a part of itself upon attack. The enemy pursues, presses on the tail, and the anole smartly responds by shaking loose, leaving behind a moving tail that distracts the aggressor while the lizard runs to freedom.

"Wait a minute," I interrupted. "You can drop the tail intentionally when attacked?"

"Well, no, it's not quite that easy," Ann said. "The anole has to struggle while something is holding the tail. The lizard tail contains vertebrae—bones like those in your own spine. Each vertebra has an area of weakness in the center. As the muscles spasm, a vertebra will fracture at the weak point. Along with it, the surrounding tissues, blood vessels, and bones separate, too. Muscles in the tail contract, causing it to twitch and wiggle like a displaced earthworm."

Tail break! The anole snaps free to escape an enemy. Tiny bones in the tail are broken. The tail twitches, distracting the enemy while the anole escapes. The tail grows back, but it is never as good as the original.

"How long can the tail move around?"

"Several minutes is not unusual," said the Professor.

"Yes, and I have seen the little lions many times pawing the wiggly tail," Noel added.

"He means cats," Ann clarified.

"Oh, of course."

"But other enemies, they will attack and chew and swallow the tail just like it was a whole anole," Noel said.

"Is it painful for the anole to lose the tail?"

"Not as painful as being eaten alive," Noel deadpanned.

We all broke into laughter at the gallows humor.

"So how long does it take to grow the new tail?" I questioned.

"Slowly is the key word," said Ann. "First, there may be a little swelling and a spot of blood. Then a scab develops and skin cells form over the stump. No longer directly connected to the spinal cord, the tail begins to attract new nerve fibers from spinal nerves close to the tail. In a couple of weeks, the new tail begins to grow in recognizable length and in several more weeks it may be close to full length."

"But it is not as good as the original," Noel argued.

"In what way?" I asked.

"The new tail will never have any bones; it's just full of cartilage and tissue," Ann said. "Sometimes, the tail doesn't break cleanly and a forked tail develops. Other times, the new tail doesn't change color like the rest of the body. The replacement tail, while not as flexible as the old one, still has some independent movement. But because it has no bones to fracture, when the tail breaks again, it tends to separate at the stump of the first encounter."

"How many times can the tail grow back?" I wanted to know.

"There doesn't seem to be a number," Ann said. "As many times as necessary."

"What shortcomings does the anole experience when the tail is severed? Is it a lost weapon?"

"No, we anoles don't use the tail as a weapon; we don't thrash it about like the iguanas or monitors do, although we can wag it a little. And we can't hang by the tail from branches like true chameleons can. But the tail is important to anoles for other reasons. Most importantly, it provides a way to balance ourselves as we climb and jump. The tail also assists in camouflage from enemies because it helps us look like a twig or vine. And the tail base is a storage area for fats that could help sustain food supplies during cold weather.

"The motto for Humies is: Never grab or lift an anole by the tail!" Ann decreed.

Magic Trait #3: The Dewlap

The dewlap is loose throat skin when relaxed. The anole tightens its throat muscles and thrusts out a bone to extend the dewlap, which is used to impress or frighten others.

The next lesson began with a song and dance that appeared to have been rehearsed. Ann and Noel in a duet to the old rock tune *Doo-Wah-Diddy*:

> *There he was just struttin' round the tree*
> *Singin' Dew-Lap-Diddy-Diddy-Dum-Diddy-Doo*
> *Colorful throat fan and that funky little chant*
> *Dew-Lap-Diddy-Diddy-Dum-Diddy-Doo*
> *He looked good; he looked fine*
> *Chasin' females all the time*

Now he's bobbin that handsome lizard head
Singin' Dew-Lap-Diddy-Diddy-Dum-Diddy-Doo
The dewlap stretched out when he wants to impress
Dew-Lap-Diddy-Diddy-Dum-Diddy-Doo...

It was very entertaining. They stepped forward in unison and back again. Noel sang lead and strutted while Ann joined in on the chorus. I applauded and whistled for an encore. Noel head-bobbed to acknowledge the audience reaction as Ann left the "stage" to formally begin the session.

"If you haven't guessed by now, *dewlap* (doo-lap) is the name we use for the brightly colored fan underneath the throat," Ann stated. Noel held his position, with dewlap extended, on Ann's command.

In its relaxed position, the dewlap is a loose throat skin that may extend all the way down to the belly, Ann explained. It folds neatly like a small packet. But when displayed, the loose skin is stretched out tight as a drum and as far forward as the snout. The dewlap is not inflated by air; rather, it is extended by a lever action of muscles and bone.

"Noel will demonstrate while I narrate," Ann said. "He first raises his head and front part of the body, straightening the front legs nearly their full length. Then he pulls back his tongue, tightens his throat muscles and thrusts out what we call the *hyoid* (hy-oyd) bone, which arches like a bow. This reveals the dewlap and all its colorful scales that are hidden when the dewlap is folded. The effect is often intensified because the dewlap is translucent, so that some light shines through."

I hollered "be right back" and went to the toolbox for a flashlight. I shined the light behind Noel's dewlap and examined it through the hand-magnifier. "It's like stained glass in a way," I commented. "As the light filters through, the scales, colors, and patterns are even more brilliant."

Ann stated that both male and female anoles have dewlaps, but that those of males are normally much larger and more colorful. Males also display their dewlaps far more frequently.

"Are the dewlaps of green and brown anoles different?" I asked.

"Good question," the Professor said. "Functionally, they are the same, but colors and markings differ. My green anole species usually has a bright red or pink dewlap with whitish scales. But, as we have seen, Noel's brown species tends to have a red or orange dewlap with a yellow border. Note the neat white edging underneath Noel's dewlap. When not extended—drop the dewlap, please, Noel—this edging is visible as a white stripe on the throat. See there?"

"So, is all this simply for looks or is there a real purpose to the dewlapping?" I asked.

"Oh, there is definitely the purpose," Noel said. "To attract the *señoritas bonitas*—the pretty ladies—and to put fear into the competitors."

"Yes," said Ann. "It's common in nature to have bright colors for threats, courtship, and to defend territory. Many bird species, for example, have colorful feathered crests on their heads that can be raised when a bright display is needed but are hidden at other times. The ability to hide the bright colors is important so as not to hinder camouflage and attract predators. The colorful area conveniently appears only when needed."

Ann explained that the dewlap sometimes functions like a long-distance billboard. A brightly colored dewlap, especially against a backdrop of dark green plants, can attract females from a distance of many yards or meters away. Dewlaps may also be used:

• To recognize a particular anole species.

• To select a partner. (Females may choose a male with the best developed or showiest dewlap.)

• As a stimulant for sexual relations.

"And to defend our territories," Noel repeated.

"How does that work?" I wanted to know.

Ann explained that the combination of dewlap extension, head-bobbing, and posturing can intimidate a smaller opponent. Size matters a lot. If the dewlap is large and imposing, the intruder may run off.

"So, the lesson is this: Whether in combat or courtship, the dewlap is definitely more than a decorative frill," I concluded.

"*Sí, sí*," Noel nodded vigorously.

Magic Trait #4: Color Change

"Based on our experience with Humies, we will bet anything that you will not answer the next question correctly," Ann gambled confidently.

"You have something to bet?"

"Well, technically, no."

"Oh ... what's the question anyway?"

"Why do anoles change color?"

"That's an easy one," I replied. "Everyone knows that. They change color to blend in with the background."

"Wrong!" Ann and Noel jeered.

"That's what everybody always says," I said defensively.

"Wrong!" they repeated.

"Then what is the answer?"

"Me, me," Noel pleaded. "Please let me make the answer."

"Yes, Noel, go ahead," Ann approved.

"These are the reasons why we change the color. Remember these three things: change in emotions; change in light; change in temperature. Emotions, light, temperature," he echoed.

"Why does everyone say otherwise, then?" I asked.

"They don't know," Noel blurted. "Remember. This is why we are telling you the facts: so you will teach the other Humies."

I nodded.

"This is what happens," Ann began. "Green anoles like me are green in color when we are active, perky, healthy, and not under severe stress. Our natural green color provides excellent camouflage in leafy trees. But if frightened, we will turn brown. Or if the weather becomes cold, we will turn brown. With the onset of

*I watched intently as each pebble-like scale
on Ann's skin began to change colors.*

darkness, we may turn brown. If ill, the skin may turn brown and be accompanied by dark spots and blotches. So when our skin color darkens, it usually means we are socially stressed, scared, cold, very tired, angry or even ill."

"Here's an example," Ann said. "Two males are bright green; suddenly one attacks the other and the weaker one instantly turns brown. Why? Because it is stressful for the overmatched anole."

"So, basically, green anoles shift from green to brown, depending on the social situation, their temperament, their well-being or the weather," I reviewed.

"They are a little more versatile than that," Ann hedged. "Color can change from a dark brown, to gray, to a greenish-yellow or bright green; but the belly usually remains white."

"Professor, you said that cold can cause color changes. How cold are we talking about?"

"In the case of green anoles, temperatures of 50° F (10° C) and lower generally cause darkening. Remember, dark pigments absorb heat better than light ones, so lizards often become darker to attract heat when they are cold and paler to repel heat when they are warm.

"Sometimes, a green anole that has turned dark brown is even mistaken for a brown anole like Noel," Ann noted.

"Well, how about Noel and the Cuban brown anoles? Can they do just the opposite—turn green from their natural brown?"

"No, we cannot be green," Noel replied. "We can be gray, black, and brown.

And many of us, we will have the yellow speckles, too. Sometimes, the powerful males, they will sit high on a perch, jet black. But when startled or scared, they will fade quickly back to brown."

"What gives us the ability to change colors?" In a word, *hormones*," said Ann. "Pay close attention now and I will describe a simplified version of what happens.

"Anoles release the hormone adrenaline from the adrenal glands, just as humans do. But in anoles, one effect of an adrenalin rush is that we turn *lighter* in color. We also have a pituitary gland—again like you. This gland releases a hormone that causes us to *darken*."

Ann said that both hormones work by changing the distribution of a dark pigment, called *melanin* (mel-uh-nin), located in color-bearing cells in the deep layer of the skin, the dermis. If the pigment is concentrated in a small part of these cells due to adrenalin, light passes through the cell and is reflected from a deeper layer. If the melanin is dispersed throughout the cells, most of the light is absorbed by the pigment, giving the body a darker, brown color.

Ann said that it may be helpful to think of these color cells as trees. When the skin is lighter, the melanin is concentrated in the tree trunk. But as melanin spreads to the upper branches, the skin becomes darker.

"Complicated," I sighed.

"Yes, but don't dwell on it. Just remember that color change is stimulated by mood, temperature and light, and that we do not change color to match our surroundings."

"And that we are not true chameleons!" Noel shouted.

"Yes," Ann agreed. "Chameleons, again, are the masters of color change. Not only do some chameleons have an extraordinary palette of colors—well beyond the greens and browns and including purples, oranges, reds and blues—they can even change bars, stripes and spots."

"Well, I think you anoles do a great job of changing colors, too," I said. "You certainly have us humans beat on that account."

"I dunno," Noel replied. "I have seen white, black, brown, yellow, and red Humies. They seem to be good color-changers."

"Um, right, Noel," I said, and did not pursue that subject any further.

Magic Trait #5:
The Convertible Back Crest

Ann said we must spend at least a few moments discussing the magical back crest that males periodically display.

Right on cue, Noel transformed himself again into what looked to me like an armored warrior, peaks rising on his back.

"We call this a *dorsal* (dor-sul) *crest*," Ann said. "Most mature male brown anoles develop this erectile crest along their neck and spine, but only the largest of the green anole males can do so."

"How does he do that?" I wondered, enviously.

"It is not difficult for me, Humie. It is just like a big wrinkle of tissue and skin. I can flex the back muscles and it pops right up."

"Touch it," Ann urged.

"Oh my gosh, it's just a fleshy thing that I can pull down or side to side. It isn't armor at all," I said, astonished. "So, if it isn't useful as a weapon, then what's the purpose?"

"It is used, along with the dewlap, to impress other males competing for territories or to attract females," Ann informed. "The male turns to the side to give the competitor a more impressive view of his extended crest and throat fan. The whole idea is deception—look bigger than you actually are. Size intimidates."

Are They Really Cold-Blooded?

"Most people think we lizards always have cold blood running through our little veins," Ann said. "But the term cold-blooded is outdated and inaccurate. The truth is, our body temperatures are often as hot or hotter than those of birds or mammals—frequently ranging between 95 and 107° F (35 and 42° C)."

Ann explained that blood circulates nutrients and oxygen throughout the reptile body, but also acts as an internal temperature regulator. As blood traveling in vessels near the body surface is warmed by the sun, it is then circulated to the center of the body. There, the heart pumps it throughout the body, spreading warmth. The opposite is also true: As blood near the surface cools, the cooler blood is spread to the rest of the body by circulation.

"Then why do people continue to refer to you as cold-blooded?"

"What they mean is that we can't generate enough internal heat using our own natural metabolism," said Ann. "Plus, we are poorly insulated. So we are forced to be *ectothermic*."

"Ecto what?"

"Ectothermic (ek-toh-thurm-ik) means that our body temperature depends almost entirely on external heat sources, especially sunshine. We need direct sunlight or indirect heat reflected from the sun. We also use solar radiation absorbed on rocks, soil and other objects."

"That's why you're basking in the sun so often."

"Precisely," said Ann. "We're always shuttling in and out of the sun to regulate our body temperatures."

"I do the same thing at the beach," I said. "Under the umbrella when it's too hot, into the water to cool off, then back in the sun if the water's too cold."

"That's the idea," said Ann.

Noel scooted over to a shady area on the patio table. Ann followed. Both said the mid-day heat in full sun was too intense.

"What happens if anoles are too hot?" I asked.

"Aiiiee!" Noel yelped, shaking his head. "This is *muy peligrosa*—very dangerous! A poor anole, he could fry like a tortilla on a sizzling sidewalk."

"He's right," Ann granted, "but more often, the anole would suffer from heat exhaustion and a severe slowdown of crucial body functions."

"And if the temperature is too cold?"

"Same type of reaction. We become sluggish and vulnerable to predators. Enzyme activity diminishes, causing digestive, circulatory, nerve-impulse and other functions to operate in slow-motion. With no enzymes to break down food, undigested items could become lodged in the gut and begin to decompose, producing enough gas to sicken or even kill the lizard. Anoles therefore have no choice but to seek shelter for survival from severe cold."

"What temperatures do you like best?"

"I think most of us here in Florida, we like the temperature between 70 and 90° degrees F (21 and 32° C)," Noel said. "This is a good range to digest the food and have the normal physical functions. During the summer, if it is much higher than 90° F, that's too hot and I go for the shade. If it falls below 80° F (27° C), then I like to bask on and off in sun and shade."

"It's important to know that everything we do is affected by changes in body temperature," Ann said. "As we reach our preferred temperature, we become more active, search for food, seek mates. When our body temperature is not in the preferred zone, we are lethargic, unable to hunt, court, digest or flee."

"We use tricks to stay warm," Noel revealed. "First, we can darken the skin color. Then we might lay on dirt or a dark rock that has been baked in the sun."

He also demonstrated how to position the body to get the most warmth. When the sun is directly overhead, anoles flatten and spread the body to expose the widest possible surface area. Earlier or later in the day, when the sun is rising or falling, they may position the body sideways toward the sun and extend the dewlap to increase their heat-attracting area.

"So, does that mean your internal body temperature is always the same as the air temperature?"

"No," said Ann. "For example, if it's 60° F (15° C) outside, our body temperature might be 15 to 20° F (7 to 9° C) degrees warmer inside. We do have some ability to retain higher internal temperatures."

The Battles of Mating Season

"Today, we are going on a good field trip," Ann announced, and our subject will be——

"*Estoy listo!* I am ready," Noel interrupted. He was darting back and forth wildly.

"Uh-hem," said Ann with a stern look toward Noel, who then settled down a bit. "And our subject will be ... courtship and mating."

"And what better time?" Noel said excitedly. "Because, now, it is the mating season."

"When did it start?" I asked.

"Mating season in Florida begins in April and lasts through early September," Ann said. "Actually, even before it begins, male anoles are scouting and establishing locations for the seasonal activities."

"That is me," Noel agreed. "I am looking in spring already for a thick shrub where I can make a comfortable home for the romance months."

I had more questions but Ann insisted we begin the outing. She had asked me to bring binoculars and a blanket. "Come along," she coaxed, skittering through the densest part of the backyard garden, among the shade-loving plants. Noel shadowed her and glanced back to make sure I was nearby. "*Siguenos, amigo.* Follow us."

When we reached a large, pink-flowering azalea bush, Ann stopped and began to speak in hushed tones. "Okay, we have entered an area heavily populated by brown anoles. I think it is better to show you what happens rather than just chat. But we must be low-key to make sure that we do not disrupt the activities. Humie, slowly and quietly spread your blanket on the ground."

I unfolded the blanket, then laid flat, belly down. I removed my binoculars from the waist holder. At just 8X magnification and with short-focus feature, the flat-black binocs were ideal for closeup activities. Ann hopped onto my left shoulder, near my ear. Noel assumed a similar position on my right shoulder.

"Now we can communicate by speaking softly, without disturbing nature," Ann said. "Let's watch quietly for a few minutes to see who is around and what they are doing."

There was some gentle rustling in the leaf litter, mulch, and twigs. We sat patiently—the three of us gazing into the brush.

Noel was the first to notice a ground skirmish. "*Allí*, there," he said in his raspy, but now low-volume voice. "A male, he is defending his home."

I could see the large male, atop a small white yard statue. His bright dewlap, a mixture of red and orange, was unfurled, and he rapidly head-bobbed and pumped push-ups like a Marine recruit.

"And there is the object of his attention," Ann said. "Another male attempting to overthrow the incumbent."

"I see the intruder," I said. This one was also dark brown, longer but slimmer than the statue male. He, too, began to bob, bounce and display. The back crest arose on both anoles like a fork from a Swiss army knife. And then they turned nearly black. Tails wagged.

"What happens now?" I whispered.

"They will see how they match up," Noel predicted. "They will compare their size and temperament. There will be a duel of the minds."

The incumbent jumped off the statue, alongside the intruder. They continued to size one another up. Then the statue lizard charged the invader, who sidestepped the aggressor like a bullfighter. The invader countercharged and the incumbent rushed back toward the statue.

"This is the mental intimidation that Noel mentioned," said Ann. "Sometimes, this lasts for minutes on end, until one decides he cannot defeat the opponent."

"And, sometimes, only a fight will decide who wins the territory," said Noel. "The warriors may even be injured and scarred. See?" Noel pointed above his nostrils, "I have a puncture here on my handsome forehead. It is from an old scuffle. Me, I think this will be one of those battles, because these seem to be two tough *hombres*."

"Are any anoles killed during fights?" I asked.

"Normally, no. There is just a struggle to see who is stronger, but usually no lost body parts and no *lagartijas muertas*—dead lizards," Noel said.

The two males turned from brown to black, erected their back crests, and battled for territory.

The anoles continued to parade and posture, but the peace process was trashed when the incumbent rammed the intruder off his legs and onto his side, however briefly. For the challenger was on his feet and retaliating instantly. Now, mouths were wide open and an intense struggle ensued.

Noel was nearly as exercised as the combatants, calling the shots like a broadcaster. "*Mira*, look, they are sparring with the mouths, trying to bite the jaws of the other. Now, their jaws, they are locked together and twisting. Oooh, now the incumbent has a mouthlock on the invader's head. There is pain on the invader's face. But the invader, he is strong, too; he has broken the jawlock and, look, he has body-slammed the incumbent."

It was a vicious battle. They rolled around like two hothead kids. I timed it on my wristwatch, and it was seven minutes before the challenger lowered his head and withdrew. His intense black color had faded to light brown as he trudged away, looking back over his shoulder cautiously every few moments.

"*Terminado!* It is over," whispered Noel. "The victor has defended his home ... this time."

"Wow, quite a battle!" I said.

"Yes, and it is just one of many challenges that the male will face in a single day or week," said Noel. "And for the season, there will be *mucho más*—many more."

"Is there time for rest?" I asked.

"Male anoles get little rest and relaxation during the mating season," said Ann. "They may lose weight because they are unable to hunt and eat regularly. They are so busy patrolling their territories, fighting off challengers, and tending to their mates that they are under lots of stress and fatigue. It has been calculated that green anole males move about 80 feet (27 meters) and average more than 100 displays each hour while patrolling their area to keep other males away. And, quite often, ultimately, the dominant male suffers from exhaustion and is overthrown and his territory conquered by a stronger, fresher male."

"Yes, but it is all worthwhile for the victor," Noel said confidently. "Look," he gestured. "There are the rewards—over to the left."

The Spoils
Of Victory

"Noel has spotted members of the female harem," Ann confirmed. "It looks like there are at least three in this territory."

I repositioned myself on the blanket, using my elbows to prop up my chin. Ann and Noel bolstered their stance on my shoulders.

"Remember our first day, we said that females maintain small territories within the male's larger domain?" Ann said. "The male will work tirelessly, fearlessly, to defend that territory, as we have just seen."

"Can the male have more than three females?" I asked.

"I myself have had up to six living in my territory at once!" Noel boasted. "But three or four is more common. If you have too many, eh, is too much work."

"And there's no jealousy on the part of individual females?"

"No," said Ann. "Not in the anole world. Females are attracted to certain male physical traits, like size, strength, and dewlap appearance. But their main instinct is simply to mate and reproduce. And to seek a home for the mating season—a secure location, as safe as possible from enemies, with an abundant food supply. The females may squabble from time to time—a sporadic chase over food or a nesting location—but these aren't serious encounters. Actually, the females live a fairly quiet life during the breeding season. They eat a lot to keep up their strength but tend to stay in their own private areas within the territory."

"So, the male has a harem and the females are without jealous instincts? Sounds superb," I commented.

"Look, here comes our conquering warrior toward the females," Ann observed. "And one of the ladies seems to be, ahem, presenting herself."

"And what does that mean?"

"She is telling the male, with body language, that she is available for mating.

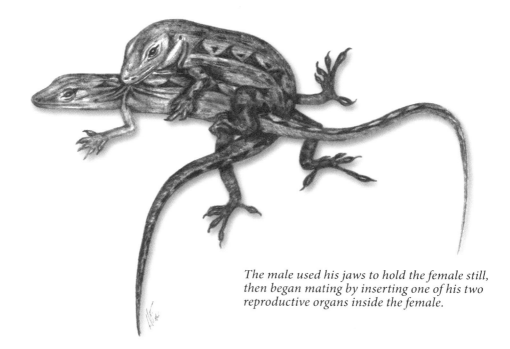

The male used his jaws to hold the female still, then began mating by inserting one of his two reproductive organs inside the female.

Females know that the resident male uses predictable trails through the habitat, so she is positioning herself in the middle of one such well-traveled roadway."

"I don't see any roads," I said.

"Well, no, they are too small and ill-defined to be identified by the untrained Humie eye, but she and the other anoles know where the trails are," Ann assured.

"Just look at her. *Ay, bonita*," Noel swooned with a rapid foot tap.

The female head-bobbed toward the male. The male lowered his throat fan and bobbed back. The female then turned her head to one side, bent her neck down and turned her posterior toward the male. The male approached from the rear, quickly clamped his jaws around her neck, straddled her by placing one hind foot over her body to clasp her leg, and slipped his tail under hers.

"That's what we call a *tail-tuck*. They are on the verge of mating," Ann whispered.

"Looks more like an attack to me!" I said. "He's displaying and head-bobbing, like he did for the fight, and now he's biting her neck."

Noel and Ann were amused. "No, this is no fight—this is romance," Ann assured. "The dewlap and head movement are used for mating, too. The male shows that he is eligible, and the female recognizes the dewlap and rhythm of the head-bob as one of her own species."

"And the biting?" I pursued.

"He is gripping the female by a fold of skin on the back of the neck," Ann said. "Anoles are just one of many lizards that do this. It prevents interruptions by holding the female still. Some females are occasionally scarred from the mating, no question. But other animals bite during reproductive activities, too. Some snakes do. Even cats sometimes do to stimulate ovulation, or release of the egg."

Ann continued, "Now, look. The male will insert one of his two reproductive organs—called the *hemipenes* (hem-eh-peens)—inside the female cloaca."

"Two reproductive organs?" I questioned.

"Yes, anole males—and other lizards and snakes for that matter—have two such organs. He will use the one nearest the side he has mounted."

Ann explained that the hemipenes are stored in small pockets in the base of the tail and are not visible until pushed out through the cloaca. When idle, they look like two tiny fingers on an inside-out rubber glove.

"Pardon the question, but why do you need two, Noel?"

"I suppose, you know, we could do okay with one, but two is better. We can mate right, or we can mate left."

Ann added that each hemipenis is attached to a separate testis (testicle). So, the male can draw life-giving sperm from one testis or the other to fertilize the female egg. Typically, the male will alternate the right or left hemipenis, ensuring that he provides the maximum amount of reproductive cells with each mating event.

Females can store sperm for up to several months, so if the male disappears and there is no replacement, she can sometimes continue to lay fertile eggs for the remainder of the breeding season.

"Is it easy to identify a male or female by looking at the genitals?" I asked.

Ann said no. "The easiest and most accurate way to determine the sex of an anole is to use at least a 10X magnifier and look for enlarged *post-anal scales* on the underside of the tail. The male has them; the female doesn't," she said. "With a little experience and a good eye, you should be able to spot them."

As the discussion progressed, so did the mating. "How long will they continue?" I asked.

"Brown anoles, like these, usually mate for 2 to 8 minutes. Green anoles frequently spend 30 to 60 minutes together."

"And how often will the male mate?"

"This varies, but typically at least once a day with at least one female. And over the course of each female's receptive period (a cycle of about six days), he will mate with everyone in the harem."

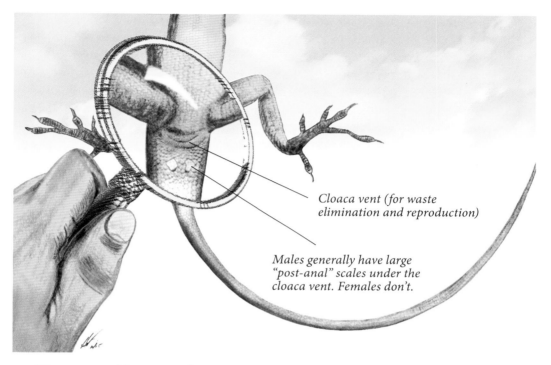

Cloaca vent (for waste elimination and reproduction)

Males generally have large "post-anal" scales under the cloaca vent. Females don't.

"Do green and brown anoles ever produce a crossbreed?" I asked.

"None that is known," said Ann. "Their chromosomes are incompatible, so even if they did have an encounter, there should be no chance of offspring."

"Look, they are finished—*terminado*," Noel announced.

The two anoles separated. There was a little head-bobbing and dewlapping on the part of the male, then both headed their separate ways.

I wanted to know what is the breeding life of the anole? Ann said that females are sexually mature at less than a year old. But for both males and females, two seasons of mating are typical.

Noel said the most exciting event is when a new female shows up. The male will drop every single activity, including the all-important territorial patrol, if an unknown female enters his home or is nearby. He will devote all of his charm and attention to attract her.

"Shhh, we have some more activity," Ann scolded. A medium-size anole skidded through groundcover.

"I think it's a small male," Ann said.

"Oh, boy, wait until the incumbent finds him in his habitat," I moaned.

"No, he's too small to be a real threat to the big male, so he will probably be ignored. The dominant male will generally tolerate small and juvenile anoles inside his territory."

She proved to be correct. Noel mentioned that, even though these small anole males are tolerated, they are not to be entirely trusted. Some are known to engage in hanky-panky with the ladies.

Ann supported his statement. "One study found that only 50% of the offspring in a typical territory of green anoles came from the dominant male. Fifteen percent came from a large neighboring male. The rest came from an unknown male or from a small male that was hiding in the territory."

"That is sneaky," I agreed. "But how did the scientists determine all that?"

"It was a very sophisticated study. They used DNA analysis of the offspring!" Ann revealed.

"Oooh, like a crime investigation," Noel said.

Greetings, World!
Birth of a Hatchling

With the field trip over, Ann led us to a comfortable park bench in the shade. She told Noel to relax for a few minutes while we discussed female issues. Noel stretched out, and Ann climbed to the top of the bench.

"What I always wanted to know before I met you two was if anoles give birth to live babies or if they lay eggs."

"And now you know the answer," she smiled. "Anoles are oviparous—not viviparous."

I guess the dumbfounded look on my face was evident. Noel got the biggest charge out of this and roared, "Ha-ha, aieee!" He was on his back with legs bucking. Ann, too, could not bite her tongue any longer and burst into laughter. What could I do but join in?

"Okay, okay," I surrendered. "I plead ignorance to your advanced vocabulary. Explain the difference."

"Female anoles are egg-laying animals, like most reptiles," Ann said, still snickering. "We call them *oviparous* (oh-vip-er-us). Other animals, like dogs or horses, are *viviparous* (vy-vip-er-us). That means they give birth to live offspring."

Noel continued to hoot. "Ha, ha, ovip, vivip . . . Humie don't know what's hip."

Ann continued, "Alright, we witnessed the mating process. Now what happens after the male has fertilized the female egg?"

She explained that the female's abdomen becomes noticeably swollen and her appetite hardier. The egg she produces is so large that it fills most of the body cavity. To handle the large egg, her ovaries alternate production: The right ovary produces one egg, which is shelled in the right oviduct. After it is laid, the left ovary and oviduct produce the next egg. The large egg can pass through her pelvic area only by being squeezed into a long, thin shape. Once exposed to air, the egg will become round again. Eventually, the egg shell becomes leathery and drier, though a little moisture can still pass in and out.

"So, she lays only one egg at a time, but how many total eggs, Professor?" I asked.

Ann said that both green and brown anoles lay on average one egg a week during the breeding season. So, if the season lasts four months, each female will lay 15 to 18 eggs. Each time she lays an egg, it is called a *clutch*. Ann mentioned that most other lizards lay one large clutch of eggs rather than a series of single-egg clutches.

"So, is this egg similar to, say, a chicken egg?"

"In many respects, yes," the Professor replied. "The egg is elliptical in shape. The embryo, or developing baby lizard, is growing inside the egg. It is protected by albumen (al-byu-min), or egg white. Attached to the embryo is the egg yolk, which is the embryo's food source. The tiny lizard embryo grows with its back to the shell and belly toward the yolk until it is developed enough to break out and live on its own."

"I'm not sure if I have seen anole eggs in the yard. What do they look like?"

"Anole eggs are off-white and about the size of the nail on your pinky finger. A green anole egg is typically ¼ inch (6 millimeters) in diameter by ⅜ inch (11 millimeters) long and weighs just 1/100th of an ounce (0.27 grams). An adult female anole typically weighs about a tenth of an ounce (2.7 grams), so each egg is equal to about 10% of her body weight."

"Does she sit on the eggs to warm them?"

"No, it isn't necessary," Ann replied. "There is no nest either. The most important thing is that eggs are laid away from direct sunlight, so they don't dry out too much. Popular spots are in damp earth or humus; in holes or cracks in rotten moist trees; beneath a rock, decomposing wood or leaf litter; in a grass clump, or maybe in between plant leaves. Even tree-loving green anoles usually come down to the ground to lay eggs."

"So, the female isn't totally indiscriminate where she leaves the egg. She thinks about it, right?"

"Well, it's more of an instinctive behavior. She first digs a hole with her snout. Then she lays the egg; if she misses the hole, she uses her snout to push it in. Then she fills the hole in. The next time she lays an egg, it may be in the same area but not in the exact spot as the first egg."

"Does the female guard the eggs to protect them?"

"No, after depositing the eggs, most females lose interest in them and the hatchling is left to chance. Neither the adult female nor the male provides any care for the eggs, other than hiding or burying them. And not all eggs hatch. Some may be eaten by other animals or attacked by bacteria or fungi."

"And how long until the egg hatches?"

"About a month."

I scratched my head. "How is it possible for the hatchlings to survive without support and teaching and direction?"

"There is no parental care provided—none whatsoever," Ann continued. "Hatchlings don't require special maternal attention as do infant birds or mammals. The little *neonate* (nee-oh-nayt)—that's what we call a newborn—is on its own. It doesn't play like a bear cub or a kitten. Even though the hatchling is less than 2 inches long (50 millimeters) from tip of snout to end of tail, it has all the necessary tools to survive. Once over 4 inches long (100 millimeters) it is considered mature. And, within a year of birth, a female anole will herself be able to reproduce."

"Gee, I assumed that the territorial male and his personal harem and the immediate hatchlings were like a family."

Ann said no. "The fact is, anoles, like most reptiles, are solitary creatures. We tend to get together for seasonal breeding and that's about the extent of our community activity. Some of the alligator and crocodile species will have the young stay near the adult for a year or so, but this is rare in the reptile world."

"There's nothing you would classify as love or family or bonding?" I asked.

"No, we really don't relate at that level," Ann said. "Just habitat, food, mating, self-preservation—those largely define our existence. Females may relocate. Or the male may be replaced by a conqueror. Our social relationships are not lifelong."

Ann said that newly hatched anoles begin eating almost as soon as they are out of their egg shell.

"Eat what?" I wanted to know.

"In the morning, you shall know," Ann guaranteed. "But we have achieved much today and I think it best to recess until tomorrow."

"*Buenas noches*, good night, Humie, *Profesora*," Noel saluted.

"Same time, same place in the morning, my four-legged friends," I waved.

As usual, Ann headed up the tree and Noel to the shrubs.

Day 4.
So What's To Eat?

Ann suggested that I eat a generous breakfast prior to lessons on our fourth day of class. "Why's that?" I asked.

"Because we are going to discuss the anole diet and have some meals, and we don't want you to feel hungry or left out."

"Maybe I'll share some of what you are having," I proposed.

"You're certainly welcome, but just in case, eat something familiar," Ann persisted.

I decided on toast, jam and melon. "Want to come inside while I eat, my friends?"

"Oh, my, that ... that would be an honor," Ann gasped. "Noel, we've been invited inside!"

"The lizards, inside the Humie habitat—I mean, house?" Noel could not believe it. "With nobody chasing us, and yelling, and trying to throw us out like a common mouse? *Sí, vamos*, let's go!"

I invited both to sit on a towel spread on the dining room table. Ann remarked that they felt right at home because the table was of natural oak. I offered them some fruit or bread, or any other foods in the household, but they declined. They were content to observe, with great curiosity, every object in their scope of vision. Lamps, chairs, pictures, candles, rugs, silverware—on and on their eyes quietly wandered. They reminded me of awestruck tourists I had seen entering centuries-old castles in Europe. I smiled, recognizing how grateful they were for the cultural exchange.

Soon I finished and said, "You have joined me for breakfast and now I will accompany you."

Both sprang from the table onto a chair and pounced to the floor, then scooted toward the back door.

"Come, Humie, come!" Noel coaxed. "We, too, are hungry."

"Another field trip, right, Professor?" I guessed.

"Correct. Make sure to grab your gear," she said.

"Binoculars," I called like a drill master.

"Check," said Noel.

"Blanket."

"Check."

"Fork and spoon ..."

"Ha-ha, aieee!" Noel wailed. "Humie, you know anoles don't need the silverwares."

I giggled along with Noel as we followed Ann around the side of the house. She chose a partly shady spot in the front yard—smack in the middle of the springy green sod, and there we laid the blanket as the base of our observation post.

"Here?" I said. "There are no bushes or ground cover or anything other than, basically, just grass."

Ann replied that anoles are versatile and will forage for food in dense shrubs but also in wide open areas.

"So what's for breakfast?" I asked.

"Bugs, bugs, and more tasty, wonderful bugs," said Noel. "Bugs with the legs, bugs with the jaws, bugs with the wings, bugs with the——"

"Alright, Noel," Ann interrupted, "I think Humie gets the idea. Yes, we anoles are *insectivores* (in-sek-ti-vors). That means we eat bugs of all types."

"No plant life? Anoles don't eat leaves or flowers or veggies?"

"No, some lizards do—like iguanas. But not us," she said.

"Our food, it must be living and lively. More to the point, it must be a tasty bug," Noel finished with a mouth-smack.

"Any particular type of bug?" I asked.

"Arthropods, in general," Ann replied. "Do you know what *arthropods* (ar-throh-pods) are, Humie?"

"Again, I have to revisit the brain attic," I said.

"Well, let me help," she offered. "Arthropods are bugs whose bodies are grouped into two or three distinct segments with jointed legs. Arthropods also have a skeleton on the outside of their body that they shed and renew."

"Okay," I said, "so that includes lots of bug types, right?"

"Yes, indeed," Ann said. "The bugs we call insects are just one type of arthropod. They have three body segments, six legs, and are the only arthropods that may have wings."

"Give me some examples of insects that you eat, then," I said.

Ann mentioned ants, beetles, and moths.

"Now, then," she continued, "the other type of arthropods that are a large part of the anole diet are the *arachnids* (a-rak-nids)."

"I know what they are. Spiders."

"Yes, for us, mainly spiders, although ticks, mites, and scorpions are also in this category. Arachnids are arthropods that usually have four pairs of legs but only two body segments and no antennae."

"And all these bugs have to be alive; you won't eat the dead ones?"

"No, we eat only live prey. We don't see stationary objects as well as moving ones. So movement is the primary way we find prey items."

"Now, *Profesora*? Now we can eat?" Noel whined.

"Yes, Noel. Seek and find."

Noel burst through the blades of grass like a trooper. He scouted the area by jerking his head from one direction to another, then bolted around a lean tree and onto a parched spot of grass. Through the low-power binoculars, I could see he had found an ant hill.

"That's certainly no surprise," Ann chuckled. "Anoles love ants, especially ant trains. Ants are easy to catch and available in large numbers. With socially active ants, it's like a buffet on a conveyor. We particularly like the plump queen ants with wings, when we can find them."

Noel continued to hunt and peck for several minutes. He returned with a look

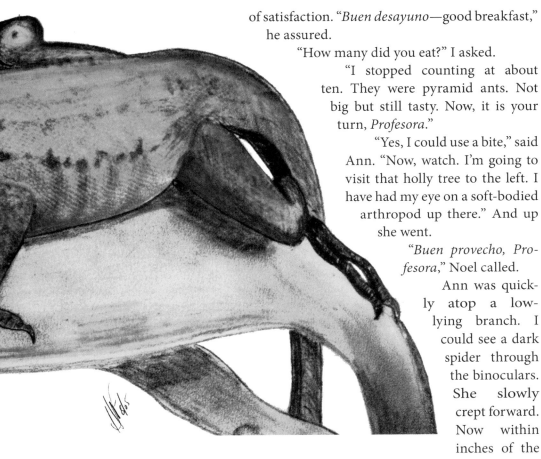

of satisfaction. "*Buen desayuno*—good breakfast," he assured.

"How many did you eat?" I asked.

"I stopped counting at about ten. They were pyramid ants. Not big but still tasty. Now, it is your turn, *Profesora.*"

"Yes, I could use a bite," said Ann. "Now, watch. I'm going to visit that holly tree to the left. I have had my eye on a soft-bodied arthropod up there." And up she went.

"*Buen provecho, Profesora,*" Noel called.

Ann was quickly atop a low-lying branch. I could see a dark spider through the binoculars. She slowly crept forward. Now within inches of the unknowing arachnid, Ann rushed with jaws agape. Spider legs wriggled from the sides of her mouth as she clamped down. Gradually, after numerous chomps, the struggling legs and body disappeared from view and Ann was on the ground by our side again.

"Green anoles like me are generally classified as *slow-stalkers.* As you saw, once we spot a bug, we inch forward until we are close enough to lunge and grab it. Noel and the brown anoles, on the other hand, often sit quietly and wait for unsuspecting prey to approach them—a method called *sit-and-wait predation.* Their brown color blends in well with the ground, making them invisible to moving prey. Once the prey gets close enough, there is a mad *dash-and-grab* before it can get away."

"So, which method is better—slow-stalk or sit-and-wait?" I asked.

"Both techniques are good, but the slow stalkers like green anoles tend to snag a few more flying insects," Ann elaborated.

"I have to try that slow-stalking a little more, then," said Noel jealously. "You know how I love the wings."

"Me, too, Noel," I said. "Chicken wings, though."

"Look, straight ahead about two feet," Ann said excitedly. "It's a small beetle."

"Then it must be Ringo," I attempted to joke, but attracted only quizzical stares.

"Please, *Profesora*, I can sample him to complete the breakfast?"

"Yes, Noel. This is a good opportunity to demonstrate close-up your technique for Humie."

Noel waited for the beetle to venture closer so that I could get a better view. He stood motionless as the doomed arthropod navigated the uneven terrain toward us. Then, as Ann had done, Noel raised the front part of his body, arched his neck, opened the jaws, and pounced. Noel struck quickly, but the beetle was so large he had to lunge forward several times to swallow it. I thought Noel resembled a dog trying to get a grip on a large bone while standing. His body and feet remained still—as if cemented to the ground—but he thrust his head and neck rapidly forward as the beetle went deeper down the hatch.

"Notice how Noel aimed for the center of the beetle. This is the most stable part of the target and has the least movement," Ann said.

"Yes, but he doesn't seem to be doing much chewing."

"Anoles don't chew that much—not nearly as much as humans," Ann explained. "The teeth are small and, though sharp, are not terribly effective in tearing prey. Rather, they are designed for grasping and holding. We use the teeth mainly to crush, puncture and perforate, but most food items are basically swallowed whole."

"Even a large bug?" I asked.

"Yes, even those."

"Why didn't he use his feet and claws to get a better grip?" I said, still fascinated by the hunt.

"Anoles just don't. Some lizards, like monitors, can use their feet to capture and even tear prey. But anoles are more likely to use only the mouth. Sometimes, though, we do use our mouths to position the prey against the ground or other object for a more secure grip."

"Does he rely much on the tongue?"

"The tongue is mainly used to manipulate the prey inside the mouth. It isn't sticky but it is moist with saliva and so is helpful in positioning the prey. Saliva also helps lubricate and soften the prey while it is being crushed."

Noel was still mashing the last of the beetle.

"So, how many meals do anoles eat each day, Ann?"

"It depends. As we said before, females eat lots to support egg production during the breeding season—up to three times more than males. The males are literally eating on the run as they continuously patrol their territories. But after breeding season—particularly from mid-September to the onset of winter—males eat voraciously, tripling their food intake. But, how many regular meals? Well, depending on how large the prey is, green anoles like me might chow once or more every waking hour."

"So you guys really do help control the bug population, don't you?"

"Just think about this factoid," Ann said. "One scientist has estimated that all of the brown anoles in a given acre of land can have as many as 60,000 bugs in their stomachs at any given moment (150,000 bugs per hectare)!"

The Food Critics' Review

"Do you two know the exact species of every bug you encounter?" I asked.

"Heavens, no," Ann said. "There are over 25,000 types of insects in the state of Florida alone. Some 5,000 species of beetles. About 250 species of grasshoppers and crickets. Over 900 species of spiders."

"I had no idea! ... Hey, I've got a thought. I'll name some common yard bugs and you two rate them—kind of like humans rate restaurant food. Say on a scale of 10."

"That will be fun," Ann agreed.

"Sí, Humie, what is the first menu item today?"

"Mosquitoes."

"Hmm. I rate them only, let's see, *uno, dos, tres*. Three maximum," Noel said. "Many times, you have to chase them around, and then when you do get them, there is not much to eat. They are too skinny."

"I can't argue with that," Ann said. "Anoles are *optimal foragers*. That means we invest a certain amount of time and energy in capturing prey, so, naturally, we want the maximum benefit in terms of size and calorie intake."

"But you do eat mosquitoes as part of the regular diet, correct?"

"Yes, but not to the extent that the mosquito population would explode if we stopped eating them," said the Professor. "In one informal study of some 200 anoles with 1400 prey items inside, there were only about three mosquitoes found. And this was in an area with a very high mosquito population."

"Next, lovebugs!"

"Yecchh!" Noel and Ann wretched. "Absolutely not." Ann insisted. "They are full of acid!" Noel pretended to cough and gag.

"What rating do you give ants?"

Ann said they are so plentiful, so effortless to catch, that, despite their small size, ants may be up to 40% of the total anole diet in some areas. She rated them a seven.

"Alright, how about spiders?"

"Aha!" Noel cheered. "Now you are talking good stuff. I give them a nine! You don't get the antennae, but you do get the eight legs, eight eyes, the chunky body, and the web-maker spiders, they have a little silk pack that, to me, is like a dessert."

"Yes, brown anoles in particular have been observed to devastate populations of web-building spiders on Caribbean islands," Ann added.

"Sounds deee-lish. But I thought all spiders were web-builders."

"No, there are non-web-building spiders, too," Ann informed. "They tend to ambush their prey on foliage or flowers. Like the jumping spider I ate this morning. Both anoles and jumping spiders are active and moving during the day, and often meet one another during hunts."

"Enlightening. How about crickets?"

"Good flavor. Meaty. Decent size. Bonus antennae. Yes, the crickets, they are a solid eight on my rating scale," Noel said.

"Crickets are just the type of soft-bodied bugs we enjoy," Ann said. "They are a staple of our diet. There are many short-winged flightless field crickets to munch on."

"And grasshoppers?"

"Yes, the smaller ones. Excellent, mmm," Noel cooed. "About the same as crickets. But not the giant ones! They are too big and the skeletons too tough."

"How about ... moths?"

"Oh, this is number 10!" Noel shrieked. "Anole ecstasy. For me, the perfect meal. You have the soft, meaty body. There are wide, feathery antenna. The legs are scrumptious. The wings cannot be compared. And there is a challenge to capture the moths, too, so it is very rewarding when you do catch one."

"Yes, moths actually have four wings which have a wonderful texture," Ann said enthusiastically. "There are scales, hairs, veins, and a thin layer of water-repellent wax. A wonderful meal."

"Sounds kind of like an artichoke," I thought. "And roaches?"

"Hmm," Noel thought. "I give them a solid eight rating. As Humies know, when you step on *la cucaracha*, the roach, it makes a big mess. For hungry anoles, that means there's a lot to eat inside—fat, carbohydrates, protein."

"Yes, we eat them up to about an inch (25 millimeters) long," Ann added. "The large Florida roaches are really more than a mouthful for anoles. Also, roaches are most active at night and we hunt mostly by day. But we do eat the small ones."

"So, as with mosquitoes, it's not as if anoles are key to control of the roach population, then."

"No, our contribution may be helpful but probably not critical. Now, the gecko lizards. They are easily the most skilled roach hunters. And if you think about it, it makes sense. Geckos are night creatures. Roaches are night creatures. Geckos are terrific climbers—even on ceilings. Roaches are great climbers. Geckos gravitate toward human habitats, as do roaches. As one herpetologist has written, 'There are few pleasures to compare with eating a well-earned evening meal in exotic surroundings while watching the local gecko population systematically eliminating bedmates [i.e., roaches].' "

"Yes, what a thrill," I deadpanned. "Anoles don't hunt at night?"

"There are rare exceptions, but mostly during the day," Ann said. "Some will set up territories near lamps and lighted windows to feed on moths and other bugs early in the evening, but we are mainly diurnal."

"Do you like centipedes?"

"In the wild, we generally do not eat soil organisms like grubs or centipedes or millipedes," Ann said.

"But the caterpillars we do like," said Noel. "And when they turn into butterflies—the small ones, anyway—we like them even better. Baby dragonflies, they are a favorite, too."

"Keep in mind that much of what we eat happens by fate," Ann explained. "Quite often, we are in our own territory and a bug of some type happens to pass through. If the bug is convenient, no matter what type it is, no matter how we rate it overall, we will generally pounce on it. That is, unless it is too large—either imposing or dangerous."

"How about food-sharing? Will one anole offer prey to another?"

"No, but there is a rather annoying habit of outright theft—one anole snatching the catch from another's mouth," Ann said.

And One More, Ahem, Menu Item

"Any other diet items we've overlooked?" I asked.

Ann cleared her throat and lowered her head. "Well, yes, there is one other—I guess you could say—controversial item."

It was unlike Ann to be evasive. "Well, what is this item?" I prodded.

"Baby anoles. Hatchlings," she said softly.

"Adult anoles eat anole hatchlings?" I said, disbelieving.

"Yes, it happens. It is certainly not the mainstay of our anole diet, but there is definitely some cannibalism and predation of hatchlings."

"Cannibalism? Predation? What's the difference?"

"*Cannibalism* is when an animal consumes one of its own species," Ann explained. "Like a green anole eating a green anole hatchling, and this does happen occasionally. *Predation* is when a member of one species—a brown anole, for example—eats a member of another species, like a green anole hatchling. That occurs much more often."

"But most of our diet is just eating the bugs, Humie," Noel said. "Take my word for it."

"Yes, Noel, but let's not understate the problem," Ann said firmly. "Scientists say that brown anoles are eating more than the occasional green anole hatchling. In fact, it is one of the main reasons there is such a serious decline in the population of our green anoles."

"But, *Profesora*," Noel appealed, "I have seen with my own eyes the green adult anoles eating our little brown ones, too."

"Yes, that happens, but not nearly as often as brown anoles eating the greens. We must take into account that your species lives in much smaller areas and much more densely, so there are naturally many more of you invaders eating more of our native green youngsters!"

Ann said that green hatchlings usually begin life on or near the ground and are defenseless against fully grown browns.

The argument was getting rather heated and personal, so I changed the subject. "Gosh, we've talked reams about solid food. But what about liquids?"

"Liquids?" Ann responded, still annoyed and a little distracted. "Uh, that's simple. Water is the extent of our pure-liquid intake. Usually, we lick it right off the plant leaves."

Anole Enemies: Staying off Their Menu

Ann led us to a pine swing hung from the ceiling on the front porch. It was a pleasant and cool location after the morning lesson. The lizards enjoyed the gentle sway.

"This morning, we learned about prey for anoles, but now we are going to spend some time discussing how we ourselves are hunted by predators," Ann said.

"I have always wondered about your natural enemies," I confessed.

"It is a challenge to survive as an anole," Ann said. "Predacious birds comb the bushes, yards and trees searching for anole meals."

"All types of birds?"

"No, some birds are mainly seedeaters, like cardinals. But others are notorious anole hunters—jays, owls, shrikes, crows, mockingbirds, herons, egrets, cranes, ibis, kestrels and small hawks among them," Ann said.

"Yes, I guess it would be difficult to outmaneuver a bird in flight."

"*Sí*" Noel said. "Many times, I have seen the shadow on the ground from above as the birds, they try to swoop on us, and I have made the escape. But, sometimes, they are clever—not flying, just walking through the grass, and we are there, too, looking for bugs. If you are trying to feed yourself, it is not always easy to think about another animal that wishes to munch you."

"Yes, food has a way of dominating one's attention," I agreed. "What other enemies do you have?"

"Snakes," Ann said without hesitation.

"Oooohhh, I should have guessed," I said. "Which kind?"

"Those that most aggressively feed on anoles," Ann said, "are black racers, corn snakes, king snakes, young rattlesnakes, pygmy rattlers, scarlet snakes, cottonmouths, and coral snakes." She said that many snakes are dietary specialists, too. Some eat only slugs, earthworms and snails. Others consume only mammals. Still others change their diet as they grow. Rat snakes, for instance, start life eating anoles and tree frogs but once bigger shift to rats, mice and birds.

"Please, *Profesora*, you know how I don't like to mention the snake creatures," Noel said nervously. He cowered behind a pot of begonias.

"When we are well-hidden in our home areas it isn't easy for predators to spot us," Ann said. "But as we venture out to hunt, find mates, or establish territories, we become easier targets. Have you ever seen an anole on a light-colored house? We really stand out."

"Any other enemies out there?"

"Other species of larger lizards are dangerous. Also, very large spiders will occasionally capture small anoles."

"And don't forget the little lions—they are a terror," Noel added hastily.

"Yes, domestic cats are fascinated by anoles," Ann said. "I have been hotly pursued by speedy cats many times, but have managed to barely escape. Sometimes, I'm sure they are just playful, but their size, claws and teeth make them a mismatch as a playmate for us."

"No, they are ruthless killers," Noel fumed. "Why they need to eat anoles—Humies serve them supermarket meals. They are not trying to survive in the wild like the birds and the snakes."

"Alright, Noel, calm down," Ann said softly. But the brown fellow remained agitated.

"The other killers are the helio-copters," he complained. "One of my harem, Fernandina, she was taking a little *paseo*—a walk—near the holly tree and she was sliced and diced. I miss Fernandina; it is a good thing I have several more females to replace her."

"He is referring to lawn mowers and weed whackers and such," I guessed.

"Yes," said Ann. "Landscaping machinery is treacherous to anoles searching for food or defending territories and unaware of the danger."

I pledged to scatter anoles by walking through trim areas before using any landscaping equipment in the future.

Ann then called for a recess before our afternoon lesson.

Black racers, mockingbirds, and other birds and snakes hunt anoles. The lizards must have thick plant coverage for hiding and protection.

Physical Prowess:
By Land, Air & Water

"I want to show you in slow motion exactly how we lizards walk," Ann said.

"I've watched you and Noel walk many times. Did I miss something?"

"Perhaps. Watch carefully. As I move my right front leg forward, I also move my left rear leg forward at the same time. Then the opposite occurs. When I step forward with my left front leg, my right rear leg moves in tandem. It's as though our legs are attached diagonally. That is why we appear to wriggle from side to side when walking slowly. It's a fish-like movement left over and improved from our amphibious ancestors long ago."

"Honestly, I never would have noticed if you hadn't shown me. But it is definitely true. It's almost like a dance step. You know how humans are obsessed with their dance crazes—perhaps a new one called The Lizard would catch the public fancy."

"I like this idea!" Noel said. "But could we call it The Anole instead of just The Lizard?"

"Ok, Humie," Ann resumed. Here is a multiple choice question for you:

Anoles are not able to:

(a) Run, (b) Jump, (c) Fly, or (D) Swim?

"What is your answer?"

"They can definitely run and jump, but I have never seen them fly or swim. I will guess (c) Fly."

"Humie, you win the contest and you have earned a prize," said Noel, sounding like a game-show host. "You will see a demonstration of a courageous loco lizard diving from a tree."

"I don't want Noel to do anything dangerous," I told Ann.

"Okay, I promise," Ann said. "Noel will not do anything dangerous." Then

Ann demonstrated how well green anoles can jump from trees. She spread her toes to help create wind resistance and slow the fall.

she paused. "I'm the one who will be jumping."

"You? No, I will not permit that, young lady!" I barked, feeling strangely parental.

"It will be fine," she said. "We green anoles do this all the time."

"Ha-ha, aiee!" Noel howled again. "*Profesora* will jump, down from the tree, and Humie will scream from fright or with glee!"

Ann ambled up her tree, past the first tier of limbs and up to a second level a good 20 feet (6 meters) above the ground. Noel and I peered skyward as she strolled toward the end of a limb.

"I'm only going to perform this stunt once," Ann projected as loudly as her petite frame would allow. The next moment, she arched into a graceful dive toward a heavily mulched area. She appeared to glide to the ground, making a soft landing, much to Noel's delight and my relief. Then, hardly missing a beat, she continued to lecture.

"Anole species like mine don't weigh much," she panted lightly. "So, when we fall, there is enough wind resistance to slow us down. On the other hand, large species—like the Knight anole, which grows up to 18 inches long (45 centimeters)—are much more apt to suffer injury by falling."

"It was breathtaking, Ann," I said. "The jump was so effortless. You looked like a parachutist easing on down."

"Thank you. You probably couldn't see much detail—me being small and the jump taking place so quickly—but I held my legs away from my body and spread my toes to increase wind resistance and slow the fall," Ann said.

"So, the answer to our question is that, no, we don't fly but small anoles are able to survive leaps from heights up to 30 feet (9 meters) without injury," Ann summarized. "Sometimes, we tree-loving anoles even use this paratrooper technique for hunting when there is tasty prey on the ground."

"Now, how about the swimming?" I asked.

"Well, there have been reports of anoles that live around the water," Ann prefaced. "Let me recite a passage about green anoles that appeared in a journal many years ago":

"Anolis carolinensis takes to water readily. If alarmed while on a bush over a pond, they sometimes jump into the water and swim away. On the night of April 24, 1934, I counted 11 of them asleep on several water-oleander bushes in the middle of a little pond...."

"So, it does happen, but the real question is: Do we like to swim?" Ann asked. "What do you say, Noel?"

"No, this is not a favorite past-time, *Profesora*. But we will do the duty if forced to."

"And when is that?" I pondered.

"If we are trying to escape from a predator," Ann revealed. "Or if we accidentally fall into a body of water. At these times, yes, we will swim as fast as we can ... to get out! This time, Noel will demonstrate."

"Me? But, *Profesora*? The air is pleasant today. I don't need the cooling off."

"Let's head to the water," Ann motioned. We followed her to my small backyard pond. There were no fish in it, but I had recently cleaned the leaves and debris, the pump was circulating nicely, the yellow pond lilies were in bloom, and the swimming conditions were above average.

Noel poked one foot into the water. "No, is too cold today, *Profesora*. We will try again—in a couple months," he stalled. Ann stared him down to show her displeasure. Momentarily, he sprang from a rock with his trademark "Aieee!" and hit the water full speed with nary a splash. And he was slick. He appeared to be almost running on the surface of the water. It was astounding how quickly he circled the pond. His lightning movements reminded me of characters from the old silent movies.

"Anole skin is very *hydrophobic* (hI-droh-foh-bik)," Ann explained. "That means we repel water. So, we paddle and swim with little resistance. Noel and the brown anoles, in particular, are excellent swimmers because their tails are fairly flat, as opposed to the green anole tail, which is rounded and therefore sinks a little, creating drag."

Ann added, "Anoles can float endlessly with hardly any movement. Basically, we are like a bag of air. Unless our lungs are filled with water, there is no reason for us to sink."

"I'm surprised that you swim and float so well and don't take a dip more often," I commented. "It would be an excellent way to help control your body temperature during the simmering summer months. There are also a lot of bugs around water for snacks."

"We have to respect predators in the water," Ann cautioned. "There might be a hungry fish or wading bird. As far as the bugs are concerned, yes, there are some juicy arthropods in wetlands, but we already have a plentiful supply on land."

Noel remained as still as a bobber on a windless day. I sat at pond's edge and said, "Hey, *amigo*, are you okay down there?"

"*Sí, es muy cómodo*—very comfortable. Maybe I will come here again. You're not going to put the fishes back in the pond, are you, Humie?"

"Only if you need some intense exercise," I jested.

"Ha, ha," Noel laughed nervously.

Track and Field Events

Ann made the transition to our next topic: running. "Who do you think is the faster of the anole species—Noel and the brown anoles or me and the greens?"

"Are we talking about marathon running or short bursts?" I asked.

"Anoles are not endurance runners. We're sprinters. So we are talking only about sprint speed."

"I'm sure it depends on whether it's a male or female and on the size and weight of the anole," I hedged.

"Yes, of course," Ann said. "But all things being equal, brown anoles are the faster sprinters." Then she gave these precise figures:

- The average adult sprint speed for brown anoles is about 5.75 feet per second (1.75 meters per second).
  - And for green anoles, 4.1 feet per second (1.2 meters per second).

I thought for a minute, then realized aloud, "That's pretty fast for a small creature! If you could sustain that speed, you could run a quarter-mile (400 meters) in under four minutes!"

"Not possible," Ann replied. "Our normal activities—like hunting, displaying, and mating—are fueled by *aerobic* metabolism, which means supported by oxygen. But, sometimes, we really have to exert ourselves because of emergencies. In those cases, our small lungs can't put enough oxygen into the bloodstream to keep up with demands for muscle energy, so we are forced to rely on *anaerobic* metabolism. And that's where we encounter major problems."

Ann said anoles use anaerobic energy for brief, intense needs, like escaping a predator. But stored energy sources are quickly and severely drained as carbohydrates are burned in the absence of oxygen. The result is rapid and overwhelming exhaustion. It may take the lizards hours or even days to recover as they replace nutrients and rebuild energy reserves.

"Yes, I've seen anoles behave like that when they wandered inside the house. After a lengthy chase to capture and then release them outside, they seemed unwilling or unable to run. I thought maybe they were playing dead, like a possum."

Ann nodded understandingly, then said with a bounce, "And now to jump—pun intended—into our final physical topic: jumping."

"You're obviously both quite good at that. How far can you jump, Ann?"

"From a perch 11 inches (28 centimeters) above the ground, adult brown anoles can leap more than 23 inches (58 centimeters) horizontally and green anoles over 19 inches (48 centimeters). To put that in perspective, that is like a 6-foot-tall (1.8-meter-tall) human broad-jumping nearly 24 feet (7.3 meters)!"

"That's Olympic quality," I said. "Where does your strength come from?"

"We get a lot of strength from our hind limbs, which are longer and more muscular than the front legs. First we flex, then we straighten to propel—not unlike humans do." Ann then climbed a tall garden trellis and made three jumps onto lower-level objects.

"Whew," she gasped, "we have had a productive session. And there's only one day of class remaining, so let's rest well tonight."

"You hear that, Noel?" I called.

"*Sí, amigo.* I will, as always, be ready to tutor."

The 5th & Final Day:
Sleep, Winters, Captivity

I was first to report Friday morning, last day of class. It had been a fantastic week learning about anoles. In fact, I thought about enrolling in some type of herpetology program later.

"*Buenas dias*, Humie," Noel greeted. "The clouds, they are many today. I think we will see *lluvia*—the rain."

"Morning, Noel. Yes, we have had perfect weather all week, but today does look a little gloomy."

"And a cheerful morning to all," Ann chirped, ignoring the threatening skies. "Today, we will complete our anole curriculum."

"What subjects do we have left, Ann?" I asked.

"A little of this and a little of that. Being that it's early in the morning, the first thing we will talk about is what we did last night."

"What do you mean, *Profesora*? Last night, we just sleep like always," said Noel.

"That's exactly what subject I had in mind," Ann said. "Because anoles are diurnal, most are awake and active when it's daylight and inactive and asleep when it's dark."

"Simple enough. But where do you like to sleep?"

"I prefer to sleep on a horizontal twig—one that's well hidden by leaves," Ann said. "I close my eyes and often place my head on another branch or leaf that serves as a support, kind of a pillow."

"I am a sound sleeper," Noel said. "I can sleep either way—sideways or straight up and down. I just need a cozy leaf, and sometimes I curl my tail back toward my head because it is comfortable and I think looks very cool, also."

"You know, many times I have seen anoles sit motionless for long periods during the daytime and thought they were sleeping. If they aren't sleeping, why are they so still?"

"That's easy," said Ann. "We sit motionless so that we can monitor our surroundings. We can observe what other anoles are doing and remain still enough so as not to frighten off any prey that might walk by."

"Also, if you see us during a very cold day sitting in the sun, usually we are still because we are not operating at full speed," Noel said.

"Which conveniently leads us to our next subject—winter activities," said Ann.

"I do wonder how you survive bitter cold days with no sun," I said. "Do you hibernate, like bears?"

Ann explained that anoles do not hibernate, but do become dormant in some ways. In true hibernation, the animal's body temperature is so low its metabolism is just barely functioning and darkness is helpful to sustain the condition. A genuine hibernating animal like a bear in a climate like Wyoming's would never be seen on a sunny day because its system has shut down for the entire winter season.

Anoles, on the other hand, experience a state called *brumation*. The drop in body temperature is not as extreme as in hibernation; the lizard is just sluggish and a period of sunlight exposure is desirable. Like many reptiles, anoles eat little or nothing during cold periods, having already built up fat reserves to get them through.

When cold fronts move in, anoles hunker down in wind-protected areas. Some find rock crevices, heavy leaf litter, or even shutters or siding on houses as a winter retreat. They usually emerge only on warm, sunny days to bask. In Florida, of course, cold periods tend to be brief, usually a few days to a week, so anoles don't need to brumate all winter. However, green anoles in much colder climates like Tennessee's are seen on sunny, south-facing rocks even when the temperature is sub-freezing. After basking, they retreat deep into fissures in rock cliffs.

"I bet you'd like to be an indoor pet during the winters, right Ann?"

"Well, since you brought up the subject, let's talk about that next."

"Captivity? Don't like it," Noel grunted. "Anoles, we are free spirits—like the eagles and whales."

"By and large, Noel is right," Ann said. "Anoles are best left in the wild. We're not the type of animal that will show affection toward the owner, and the average anole is not terribly trainable. Oh, you may find one that will eat from the

Noel, a free spirit, was opposed to cages and captivity.

owner's hand, but that's about it. Still, anoles are probably the most popular pet lizard in the entire U.S.A., so we should spend some time outlining how to care properly for those in captivity."

"If you do not mind, *Profesora*, I am going out to hunt in the wild while you talk about prison life." Ann nodded and Noel disappeared into a tangle of jasmine.

"Why are anoles such popular pets then, Ann?" I asked.

"We are fairly easy to catch, and small enough that a youngster can take care of us. We're kind of a starter lizard for budding herpetologists. As reptile lovers become more serious, they often graduate to larger, exotic lizards, like iguanas."

"So, if someone in, say, New York wants an anole, where does he get one?"

"Pet store," Ann replied. "But in a state like Florida, people just capture anoles in the wild. Be advised, however, that it is legal to collect only brown anoles and not the native green species. Humans, especially kids, can usually chase down an anole pretty quick. But I have seen more sophisticated techniques used as well."

"Like what?"

"Some researchers use a noose with light fishing tackle or even dental floss on a short pole. They sneak up behind the anole and gently draw the noose tight around the neck. That's one method. I have also seen a night invasion."

"Sounds sinister."

"Not really. Just snatching sleeping anoles from leaves at dark."

"Is there any kind of danger when handling anoles?" I asked.

"No, not normally. You'll probably get bitten—especially by aggressive males— but, of course, we usually can't break the skin and do no harm. Uh, you may also get pooped on, heh-heh. If you see a little brown kernel with a white tip, then you have been victimized."

"Certainly understandable, with all the stress," I said. "Okay, so now that an anole has been captured, how do you take care of it?" Ann asked me to be seated while offering these basic instructions:

• **Cage**: Use a large ventilated enclosure. Allow at least 10 gallons (38 liters) for one anole, and add another 10 gallons for every two additional anoles. She pointed out that a cage for reptiles is called a *vivarium* (vy-ver-e-um).

• **Furnishings:** Provide lots of branches, bark, and vegetation for climbing, basking and hiding. Add some greenery for relaxation and perching. Live plants help maintain high humidity. Ferns, spider plants, bromeliads and ivies are good choices. A few plastic plants can also be used for cover. Sphagnum peat moss is popular for the cage bottom. Spot-clean daily to remove wastes and clean the vivarium thoroughly every month or so.

• **Temperature:** Use an incandescent light with reflector to heat the cage. During the day, regulate the temperature at 75 to 85° F (24 to 29° C) with a basking zone of about 90° F (32° C) for up to 12 hours. At night, for the remaining 12 hours, reduce the temperature to 70-75° F (21-24° C). If night-time heating is necessary, use an infrared nocturnal reptile lamp. Do not use a white or bright light because this will disrupt the lizard's sleep cycle and result in stress. Maintain the humidity at 50-80%. During winter months and the brumation period, some owners suggest lowering the temperature 5 to 10° F and reducing the humidity by up to 20%. The reduced temperature can be achieved using a lower-wattage bulb in the reflector lamp and reducing the daylight hours from 12 to eight. A timer is a good idea to make sure that lights are turned off during the night and on during the daytime.

• **Lighting:** Install a fluorescent lamp with ultraviolet (UV) wavelengths to supply simulated sunlight. A good UV lamp will provide UVB rays to prevent bone disease, as well as UVA rays to promote healthy appetite, physical activity, and psychological well-being. Do not use window light alone! This will result in poor bone development and other serious problems as the window glass filters out the essential UV wavelengths.

- **Population:** Just one anole is suggested. This way, you can concentrate on anole care without creating social problems. Do not house male anoles together! They will fight, and the weaker one will likely die from the bullying. If you have one male and one or two females in a small space, the male will tend to chase and stress the females, especially during breeding season. And, of course, eventually you will have a bunch of baby anoles. If you must have two anoles, try two females. With no males around, stress will be reduced, eating will be easier, and there will be no population boom.

- **Hatchlings:** If you do end up with eggs, you can incubate them in a cup filled halfway with moistened vermiculite. Put the eggs on top of the mixture and return the cup to the cage, controlling the temperature at 75 to 90° F (24 to 32° C). Eggs should hatch within about 35 days. Once hatched, place the youngsters in a separate cage in case you have a cannibalistic adult. Feed the hatchlings as many pinhead-size crickets or wingless fruit flies as they will eat.

- **Water:** Use a spray bottle to provide a daily misting of the vegetation or offer a dripping water supply.

- **Feeding:** Crickets are a good soft-bodied food that can be purchased at many pet stores. They and other food items should be dusted with calcium lactate and other vitamin/mineral supplements to provide proper nutrition. Feed the anole daily, offering only as many prey items as it will consume in 5 minutes. Mealworms (larvae that metamorphose into beetles) are also cultured for lizard food, are rich in amino acids and proteins, and are a good occasional food alternative. However, if mealworms are old and dry, they can clog anole intestines.

- **Commitment:** Pet-store owners say the biggest problem is that many children lose their enthusiasm and parents end up caring for anoles, as well as other pets. Realize that any pet requires a long-term commitment.

Noel suddenly reappeared, and Ann commended him on his timing. She said the day's lesson was drawing to a close and that she needed to make a special announcement.

The Unexpected Announcement

Ann asked both Noel and me to sit down. She had a very serious expression on her face.

"Okay," I said, "I'll relax in the rocker and Noel will join me." He nimbly trekked up my elbow and onto my chest. Up against my yellow pullover shirt, he looked like a three-dimensional apparel icon. Very smart.

Ann stepped to the center of the table. She cleared her throat and spoke slowly.

"Ahem ... it has been my honor, privilege and pleasure this week to tell the anole story. Never before have we been able to communicate at this level with humankind. And it has been a delight each day to welcome an eager, devoted student who respects our species and way of life."

Noel cheered, "She is talking about you, Humie! You, the eager one."

"Yes, Noel, thank you," I acknowledged modestly.

"But now my task—our task, for Noel and me—has been fulfilled. And I want to announce that our gift of advanced communication and verbalizing is, well, only temporary."

"You mean that, gulp, you won't be talking anymore, Ann?" I said meekly.

"I'm afraid that's exactly what I mean," Ann nodded. "Noel and I were temporarily empowered to educate the human race, but now our powers are about to expire."

"*Profesora*, this I did not know!" Noel was astonished.

"Yes, Noel, I couldn't share this information with you earlier. We had a job to do, and I could not have you worrying about loss of newfound skills."

"Ann, will we still maintain our relationship? Will you continue to know me? Will you come by to visit each day? Or for meals?"

Slowly, steadily, she shook her head no. "Tomorrow when we wake, we will revert to ordinary wild anoles, unable to talk, wary of the presence of humans, consumed by the duties of our separate anole species."

"Ann, if what you say is true," I pleaded, "I can make a grand vivarium where you can live as my guests or pets or whatever you want to call it. I'll feed you and clean your pen and care for you so that you will never have to worry about hunger or predators or harsh weather."

"That is so thoughtful," she replied. "But we are wildlife and we must return to the ways of the wild. It is better to face danger amid the challenges of life than to live safely and securely but without purpose as a captive."

"She is right, Humie," Noel conceded. "Even with a kind person like you as caretaker, still I would be restless and depressed in a cage."

I was grieved, but I understood their position. I wouldn't want to be held captive against my will either. I managed another question.

"Ann, where will you go? Will you at least live here in my yard?"

"I will not. I will be relocating far away."

"But, why? Don't we have everything you need here in the yard? Food, water, pleasant weather?"

"*Sí*, where you will go, *Profesora*?" Noel echoed.

"I must go north. There are dwindling numbers of my species here in the central and southern portions of the state. This year, many of us were unable to find new mates. No breeding, no population, no future. I will just head north. And when I find the right habitat, with a thriving population of my species, that will be it. I will join the other green anoles in areas less heavily populated by the brown anoles."

"I am very sorry, *Profesora*," Noel murmured. "I wish I could persuade my brown *amigos* to be less aggressive so that our green brothers and sisters can—"

"It's not your fault," Ann interjected. "It's no one's fault in particular, Noel. It's just fate. I have to deal with it as do many of my species."

"Ann, is there nothing I can do to make life here more comfortable for you and your kind," I said.

"Well, no. Not really. That would require a major habitat change. A lot of trouble …"

"Try me!" I pleaded. "What would it take? If there is something I and others can do to assist our native green anoles, then we Floridians ought to know about it? That's what we're here for—education, right?"

"*Sí, Profesora*," Noel agreed. "*Diganos.* Tell us, for the class."

"Yes, of course, education," Ann sighed. "But our habitat requirements seem to go against the human concept of, uh—I guess you'd say—yard beautification."

"How so?"

"Well, here is our situation." Ann sounded close to sobbing. "As you know, the brown anoles have invaded our state, and our green anole population has been ravaged—probably by 90%. Where there is little vegetation, both species seem to compete for living space and food items. But the brown invaders populate so rapidly, hunt so fiercely, and now you know they also eat some of our young. They have forced us green anoles to higher habitats, and we accept that. If only we had more trees and tall shrubs with camouflage, leafy protection, and food sources, then I believe we could survive in our traditional areas throughout Florida."

She struggled to continue.

"The problem is that Humies prefer plain grass lawns. Around their homes, their businesses, their developments, their cities, they continue to eliminate our habitat. They remove most trees and tall shrubs, replace them with manicured turf grass, and then surround everything with cement or asphalt."

"Ann, you mean I and others could help green anoles simply by planting more tall, dense vegetation?" I said.

"Yes, trees and native Florida plants and tall shrubbery and vines. This would give us a fighting chance to repopulate our native territories. No, we will never be as numerous as we once were, before the invaders. But without tall, thick vegetation, we have no chance whatsoever."

"So, you're saying that, with proper plant life, you and Noel, the greens and browns, could actually live comfortably, even on the same premises?"

"Yes, it's a fact. In Cuba, the Bahamas and elsewhere in the Caribbean, browns and greens have evolved together. They continue to live—often thrive—in the presence of each other. The greens simply perch above the browns. Why not here in our home state, too? The only thing missing is sufficient vegetation."

"Ann, how much time do we have left until, uh, you know, we can't communicate anymore?"

"Well, it is almost noon and our powers will wind down at dark."

"Then we have no time to waste. Let's go shopping."

"Shopping for what, *amigo*?" said Noel.

"For habitat!" I said, pounding the table for emphasis. "Ann stays!"

The Quest
For Habitat

We were in the pickup truck and on the road within an hour. The three of us on the front seat—Ann and Noel in an old aquarium furnished with pine bark, ferns, and twigs.

"Where are we headed in such a frenzy?" Ann asked.

"I just made some phone calls to a large nursery. They sell lots of plants native to this state. Plants that you know and can help select for your very own habitat, in my yard. Which is where you belong, Ann."

Ann tilted her head and looked into my eyes using the monocular vision of her left eye. "You would do that for me?" She was clearly moved.

"Just watch and see."

"He is so dedicated, is he not, *Profesora*?" Noel said.

"I have sketched out the current yard plan on this pad. See this, Ann? Next to it, I have listed some native Florida shrubs and trees that will grow well in our area of the state. I got those out of my gardening book. In particular, I want your suggestions about which plants to put where for your well-being. Noel, you are welcome to contribute as well, but, remember, our main purpose is to reestablish Ann's community."

Noel nodded emphatically.

"Gosh, it has been so long since I have even seen some of these specimens," Ann said longingly. "Ah, what it would be like to wander through a tall Walter's viburnum shrub once again," she imagined. "Lovely white flowers in the spring. Dense cover. They grow so well in the full sun or even partial shade."

"Who is this Walter guy?" Noel questioned.

"That's just the name of the plant, Noel," I answered. "It's not necessary to know who Walter is just now."

As we pulled into the nursery on the outskirts of town, I told my scaly comrades to ready themselves. I parked on the dirt driveway and put on my straw Bahama hat with red bandana wrapped loosely around the center. "Now hop on, friends," I commanded. Both jumped onto the front brim. "Please stay behind the bandana and keep your voices down when we see staff or shoppers. I don't want anyone hauling me off to an asylum for talking to lizards. Nor do I want anyone hijacking my talented reptiles as a carnival act."

"Yes, of course," Ann said. "We will hide and talk low."

"I think the carnival would be fun," Noel countered.

"Hush!" said Ann.

I then placed the hat on my head and marched with purpose toward the vast nursery fields. A lean, elderly, tanned attendant greeted me. I told him I was interested in tall, bushy plants or small trees that are easy to grow and require little care. He courteously led me around the property, citing pros and cons of the many Florida species. Ann and Noel stayed out of sight.

"Now, this here American beautyberry grows seven or eight feet tall, gets some pretty purple flowers couple times a year, and likes part-shade. Just keep it in well-drained soil. Also got, here, the fetterbush, firebush, and gallberry—all Florida species that get nice and thick and tall. Then he led us to more shrubs and to native groundcover plants and trees. I thanked him for the orientation and told him I needed some time to decide. "No problem," he answered, "just yell when you're ready to load 'em up."

Ann was thrilled with the selection and had already settled on several plants. As she dictated, I jotted down her choices. Soon the truck bed was full and we were ready to head out.

I lowered the straw hat toward the aquarium and the anoles hopped in. Ann was chattering nonstop about the new acquisitions—where to put them, how tall they would grow, how to care for them. Noel could hardly get a word in.

"Oh, the yaupon hollies—I know just the place for them! On the west side of the house, near the privacy fence. They are going to grow 10 to 15 feet high (3 to 4.5 meters). There will be thick leaf cover—camouflage and protection and habitat for us green anoles."

"Leaves in winter too, *Profesora*?" Noel inquired.

"Yes, the yaupon holly is an evergreen, Noel. Its leaves will stay green year-round."

She prattled on again. "The Simpson's stopper is another hefty bush, and it

We searched the nursery for plants that would provide good habitat for Ann and other green anoles. I told the lizards to stay behind the bandana when the attendant came by.

is going to be up to 12 feet (3.6 meters) tall. It can be trimmed as a hedge or just allowed to grow freely. It also blooms wonderful, fragrant, little white flowers. And the wax myrtle, with its bluish, waxy leaves, is another bushy native evergreen that can grow to the size of a small tree. The saw palmettos and muhly grass will grow at a lower level, up to 4 feet (1.2 meter), but all will work together to restore our native habitat for dwelling, mating, and hunting. The other benefit is that these beautiful Florida plants can be planted in sun or shade and do not need regular watering, once established."

"That's right," I said, "the nursery guy used the expression *drought-tolerant*. They are hardy plants that eventually require little irrigation or human care."

"If builders and home buyers would just clear less vegetation from new residential and commercial building sites," Ann imagined. "Just think of the benefits. There would be less grass to take care of. That means less fertilizer

Ann dreamed of more yards friendly to green anoles—less grass, tall shrubs, and more trees to provide protection and living space above the invader brown anoles. ▶

and pesticide would be used, so runoff and pollution would be reduced. There would also be much less impact on our precious water resources. Did you hear what the nursery man said? Over half of the drinkable water consumed in our state is used just to irrigate lawns!

"And, of course, there would be far more natural habitat for our native green anoles," she said.

"And a lot less lawn mowing!" I cheered.

Ann emphasized that native plants, in particular, should be favored. She said certain non-native plants are *invasive*—that is, they monopolize the land and displace the native plants. This can harm wildlife that has evolved to depend on native plants for food and shelter.

The Lizards
Wind Down

It was close to dusk when we finished the landscape plan. Ann had the ability to foresee how the young plants would grow and occupy space in the months and years to come. I labeled the spots where I would physically plant everything over the next few days. I further surprised Ann with a young Southern magnolia tree I had secretly brought home from the nursery, hidden among her selected plants. She was speechless.

"This tree," I decreed, "will be known as the Ann Tree. It represents my efforts to create natural living conditions that will attract native green anoles to this yard, to this neighborhood, and to this area of our state. When someone comes to my yard, I will always tell him or her that this is not just a magnolia tree, but a symbol to reestablish the green anole in its rightful domain."

Ann peered on proudly, while Noel stood by respectfully.

For the next two hours, we enjoyed one another's company. I wanted to review some of our lessons and had a few more questions. Noel continued to chitchat. Ann was remarkably at ease, considering that she was on the threshold of major life changes. But as the muted sun dissolved on the overcast horizon, it was clear that my pals were beginning to tire.

I wanted both to rest peacefully for the night before their release to the wild, so I set up the aquarium again. I covered the top with screen held tight by bungee cords. But then I thought: We've got a problem. After dark, Ann and Noel will not get along. One green anole, one brown. One male, one female. I promptly partitioned the aquarium using a piece of plywood.

I asked Ann if she was ready to turn in. "Yes, very soon," she said soberly. "But first I have to know, Humie. All the information, the lessons, the field trips, the conversations. How will you convey this information to other Humies? Have

A Glance At Those

Green Anole

Scientific Name
Anolis carolinensis
("Carolinensis" refers to the Carolnas, perhaps where specimens used to classify the species were found by scientists long ago)

Original Native Range
Florida (sub-tropical region) and other deep southern states

Current U.S. Range
Mostly throughout southeastern states; also in portions of North Carolina, Tennessee, Texas, Oklahoma, Hawaii

Behavior
Shy, mild disposition

Body Shape
Head and body slender; shorter legs but longer toe-pads than browns

Total Length (tip of snout to end of tail)
Males: up to 8 inch (203 mm)
Females: up to 5 inch (127 mm)

Body Length (excluding tail), called "Snout to Vent" Length
Males: up to 2 3/4 inch (70 mm)
Females: up to 2 1/3 inch (60 mm)

Habitat
Trunk-crown species. Mainly in tall, thick shrubs, upper tree trunks, and leafy areas of trees (called the crown or canopy)

Predatory Style
Slow-stalker. Creeps along slender branches looking for prey

Color Range
Natural green color provides cam-ouflage in tree canopy. Can change to greenish-yellow, brown (including dark brown), and gray. Belly is white.

Throat Fan (Dewlap) Color
Brilliant red to pink with whitish or red scales. (In South Florida, dewlap may be gray, nearly white or pale green.)

Pattern on Skin, Males
Generally none

Pattern on Skin, Females
Many, but not all, have light vertical stripe down back

Life Span
Up to 2 to 3 years in wild; 3 years or longer in captivity

Florida Yard Lizards

Cuban Brown Anole

Scientific Name
Anolis sagrei
(Named after Ramon de la Sagra, the great 19th-century Cuban naturalist)

Original Native Range
Cuba, then transported to other areas of Caribbean, Central and South America

Current U.S. Range
Mostly Florida, along with sections of Georgia, Louisiana,Texas and Hawaii

Behavior
Aggressive, bolder than greens

Body Shape
Bigger, shorter head; longer legs but smaller toe-pads than greens

Total Length (tip of snout to end of tail)
Males: up to 7 inch (177 mm)
Females: up to 5 inch (127 mm)

Body Length (excluding tail), called "Snout to Vent" Length
Males: up to 2 3/4 inch (70 mm)
Females: up to 2 inch (52 mm)

Habitat
Trunk-ground species. Mainly low on tree trunk, in low shrubs, and on ground

Predatory Style
Sit-and-wait. Tries to be invisible to moving prey

Color Range
Natural brown color provides camouflage around tree trunk. Can change to dark brown, pale gray, dark gray, or black. Yellow or white speckles common.

Throat Fan (Dewlap) Color
Reddish or reddish-orange with yellow or cream-colored border and white edge

Pattern on Skin, Males
Numerous patterns possible. May be banded or spotted; may have light keel down back; may have chevrons ("sergeant stripes"), etc.

Pattern on Skin, Females
May have diamond-shaped pattern down back; dark scalloped shapes; light, vertical wavy stripes; many other markings

Life Span
Up to 2 to 3 years in wild; 3 years or longer in captivity

you thought about that?"

"Of course, Ann. At first, I thought an article in the newspaper or local magazine would be enough. But with all of the details you have given, there is only one possible answer."

"And what might that be?" Ann asked anxiously. Noel's interest peaked as well.

"A book!"

"Hurrah," cheered Ann, "a book!"

"We'll be as popular as Snoopy the Beagle, Nemo the Fish!" a drowsy Noel mustered as excitedly as he could manage. "And then there will be the movie rights. Who will play the role of Noel?"

I cupped my left hand and told my friends to climb on. As I walked toward the cage I stroked their backs with my forefinger. They were growing quieter by the moment. I spent several minutes petting them and repeating that our relationship was unforgettable and that I wouldn't let them down. They offered a few words of encouragement but were like two worn batteries in a dimly lit flashlight.

As the last bit of daylight expired, it began to drizzle and I lowered my companions into their private chambers. Noel trudged onto a fallen green leaf upon a heap of bark. Ann shinnied up and clasped her leg around a thin branch. There were no further remarks, as both dozed off quickly. I lowered the screen lid, recognizing that my learned friends would soon be completely transformed.

The Day After: Release, References, Hearsay

I slept restlessly and hurried to the cage at dawn. As she had predicted, Ann was now as untamed and free-spirited as any other anole. It didn't stop me from talking to her, though. All the while I hoped for a reply but none came.

I scooped her out of the aquarium with a net and carried her to the base of the elm. I took a deep breath, sighed, and, reluctantly, gently turned over the net. She walked forward tentatively. Her color was off, indicative of the stress of captivity. As I released her, she did not look back. But I took satisfaction as she did what arboreal lizards do—scaled the tree, disappearing among the brawny limbs. Tears welled in my eyes, those of sorrow but also those of happiness. She would be staying in my yard. Her yard. Our yard.

Noel was in a foul mood, feisty and combative, which was certainly normal for an energetic male in confinement. I wanted to identify him, at least for a short while, so I used a soft-tip pen to write an "N" (for Noel) on his right side. This would be sufficient until he shed his skin. Some scientists, Ann had told me, actually clipped different combinations of toes for ID purposes, but I had no intention of tormenting or disfiguring my dear friend! He said goodbye, in his own way, I guess, by snapping at my finger two or three times.

"Okay, Noel, back to your habitat," I commanded. He bolted out of my hand and toward the home shrub. I felt good about Noel's release, too. He was in familiar territory.

The rest of the day, I readjusted to life without my mentors. First I checked the public library for anole references. The oldest I found was written in 1709 and described *Anolis carolinensis*:

"They are of a most glorious green, and very tame. They resort to walls of houses in the summer season, and stand gazing on a man, without any concern or fear."

This passage was written by J. Lawson in *A New Voyage to Carolina*.

Later I decided to ask questions of those I knew and didn't know about those Florida lizards.

First, the mailman came by. "Say, Jeff," I said, "you know these lizards all over the yards around here. You know what kind they are?"

"Must be chameleons," he said with reasonable assurance. "Why do you ask?"

"Just doing a little research," I replied. "Ever had any interesting experiences involving them?"

"Well, I've accidentally decapitated a few. Sometimes I lift up the mailbox lid and there are lizards inside; they seem to pop their heads out about the same time the lid drops down," he said nonchalantly.

"Oooh," I moaned.

"They are chameleons, aren't they?"

"No, no. Actually they're called anoles."

"Never heard of those. Well, got to finish the route." And he waved so long.

Later, I received a call from a business associate. Somewhere toward the latter part of the conversation I mentioned, "Dave, you know those lizards we've all got in our yards?"

"You mean the salamanders that jump from plant to plant?"

"Yeah, but they aren't salamanders; they're called anoles."

"That's a new one on me."

"Know any interesting stories about 'em?" I asked.

"Well, I'll tell you this. I've got a hunting dog in the back yard, and every now and then he goes into point position at the lizards. That's when I know it's been too long since I've had him out bird hunting."

This time, I thought, I'll contact a genuine lizard authority. But who to call? Got it, the herpetology center at the zoo. I tracked down the number in the phone book and was forwarded to a gentleman by the name of Nick.

"Nick," I explained, "I've got some questions about these small lizards you see all over the yards here in Florida."

"Those are just common anoles," Nick said indifferently. "If you really want to see some exotic lizard specimens, come on over and I'll show you rainbow whiptails, emerald swifts, Amazon racerunners, bearded dragons and other species from all over the world."

"I intend to do that, but right now I'm just trying to find information on anoles," I said. "Got any facts of interest or anecdotes about them?"

"Hmm," he thought. "Like I said, they are just ordinary anoles. But there is one thing that tickled me. I used to work for a reptile theme park—you know, the one with all the alligators? Well, lots of European tourists spotted anoles on the property and actually thought they were baby alligators!"

"That is funny," I agreed. "So, some folks think they're Gators, even though they're really 'Noles," I joked, referring to the football rivalry between the University of Florida Gators and Florida State Seminoles. Anybody else I might talk with about anoles."

"Let me think … yeah. There's a guy who works for the state. Name's Paul Moler. He knows a lot about reptiles. I'll give you his number."

I reached Paul later that day. I asked exactly what he did with the state. He gave his title as basically snake and lizard specialist at the Florida Fish & Wildlife Conservation Commission.

"Paul, the zoo people say you know lots about lizards and I am interested in these anoles we see in our yards all over the state."

"Yes, I am familiar with anoles. What is it you'd like to know?"

"What I'm trying to find out is if there are any interesting stories—say, folklore about them."

Paul paused briefly. I was thinking, no doubt this seasoned herpetologist is reflecting on his decades of formal education and field experience in order to furnish an expert reply. And then the answer came, "Folklore? No, not that I'm aware of. You see, the trouble with anoles is that they never learned how to write, so they have never recorded their folklore."

"Thanks, Paul."

Later, through a contact at *The Orlando Sentinel* newspaper, I learned that anoles were the inspiration behind a major contribution to the Central Florida arts. In the year 2000, artists created nearly 80 anole-like characters, which were displayed throughout downtown Orlando sidewalks, parks and buildings to promote the arts. These comical fiberglass masterpieces were 5 feet (1.5 meter) tall. Characters included The Long Tail of the Law (police-anole), Harley Lizardson (biker-anole), Frank Lloyd-Lizard (architect-anole), and the Wonderful Lizard of Oz (self-explanatory anole). In addition to drawing to downtown Orlando hundreds of thousands of art lovers, each piece of LizArt was eventually sold at an average price of more than $3,000, for a total of over a quarter million dollars.

That night, I had a dream about anoles. I thought it was significant because it typified the identity crisis they have. It went something like this:

"Knock, knock."

"Who's there?"

"Anole."

"An 'ol what?"

"Anole lizard."

"How old of a lizard are you."

"I didn't say I was an old lizard; I said anole lizard."

"So you got a Southern accent. Same thing. An old lizard, an 'ol lizard. How old are you?"

"I'm 18 months old. About middle-age for anole lizards."

"I don't care what kind of lizard you are. A year and a half doesn't make you an old lizard in my book!"

"Alright, let's start over. Forget about age. Forget about old lizards or young lizards. I am a lizard. I am of a lizard species called the anole. Spell that a-n-o-l-e."

"I don't see the difference: You say an ole lizard, I say an ol' lizard. Hey, you're not really a chameleon are you? You sure look like a chameleon to me."

"You know, you are really a good prospect for a book called *Anoles: Those Florida Yard Lizards*. Have you heard of it?"

"No, can't say I have. Is it an 'ol book or a new one?"

Cheers and Special Thanks

To the following Lizard Wizards for their invaluable input:

• Todd S. Campbell, PhD, Asst. Professor, Dept of Biology, University of Tampa, Tampa, FL. *(Note: Dr. Campbell deserves extra credit for influencing the ending of this book to promote a positive solution to the plight of the native green anole.)*
• Thomas A. Jenssen, PhD, Professor, Dept. of Biological Sciences, Virginia Tech University, Blacksburg, VA
• Julian C. Lee, PhD, Professor of Biology, Emeritus, Biology Dept., University of Miami, Coral Gables, FL
• F. Wayne King, PhD, Professor & Curator of Herpetology, Florida Museum of Natural History, Gainesville, FL
• Paul Moler, Biologist, State of Florida Fish & Wildlife Conservation Commission, Gainesville, FL
• Kurt Schwenk, PhD, Professor, Dept. of Ecology & Evolutionary Biology, University of Connecticut, Storrs, CT
• Jonathan B. Losos, PhD, Dept. of Organismic & Evolutionary Biology, Harvard University, Cambridge, MA
• Kenneth Petren, PhD, Assoc. Prof., Dept. of Biological Sciences, University of Cincinnati, Cincinnati, OH
• William E. Cooper, PhD, Professor, Dept of Biology, Indiana University-Purdue University, Ft. Wayne, IN
• A.C. Echternacht, PhD, Professor, Dept. of Ecology & Evolutionary Biology, University of Tennessee, Knoxville, TN
• Kellar Autumn, PhD, Assoc. Prof., Dept. of Biology, Lewis & Clark College, Portland, OR
• Neil Greenberg, PhD, Prof. of Ecology & Evolutionary Biology, University of Tennessee, Knoxville, TN

Note: Mention of the above Lizard Wizards does not in any way imply that they have either read or endorse this publication. This is just a show of gratitude for putting up with my persistent questions.

Credits Department

- Special thanks to Central Florida graphic artist Henry Flores (henryfloresgraphics. com) for a superb job on the illustrations. Henry was always good-natured during our many productive brainstorming sessions. For the longest time, I thought he was as nocturnal as a gecko, but later found he can work days, too. A commercial graphic artist and illustrator, Henry is equally skilled with computer-generated graphics and traditional pencils.
- Also must acknowledge the indispensable all-around help from friend and graphic designer Chip Riggs of Generation 3 Studios (gen3studios.com). Multi-talented Chip offered many tips on all phases of this project, including editorial, design, computer applications, and printing.
- Now to those wonderful folks who were courageous enough to critique the rough manuscripts and offer suggestions: Ike Flores, former Associated Press writer/editor; David Wilkening, writer; Richard Campbell of Charlotte, NC; Dr. Richard Poole, retired plant physiologist; Neta Villalobos-Bell, environmental educator; Marianne Popkins, museum director; Randy Snyder, naturalist; Mary Keim, biology instructor; Bill Belleville, author; Jack Webb, librarian; Penny Cechman, science teacher; Nick Clark, zoo reptile keeper; Jim Thomas, native plant specialist; Greg Pikulski, valued friend, Alpharetta, GA; Nicole Bremiller, a young reviewer from Sauquoit, NY; and Debra Bremiller, my best, favorite, loving and harshest critic for not only tolerating, but consistently encouraging, my offbeat idea to write and publish this book.
- Other: David Drylie, landscape architect; Mark Deyrup, PhD, biologist/author; David Burna, a neighbor who, coincidentally, knew a lizard expert; Les, Valerie, and Sarah "Mini Val" Parks (lizard catchers); Eric Schmidt of Harry P. Leu Gardens; and Teresa Watkins, native landscape educator.
- Geographic boundary for map on pages 26-27 from *A Field Guide to Reptiles & Amphibians of Eastern & Central North America,* Roger Conant et al., Houghton Mifflin, Boston, MA, 1998.
- Superman is a registered trademark of DC Comics.
- Spider-Man is a registered trademark of Marvel Characters.
- Snoopy is a registered trademark of United Feature Syndicate.
- Nemo is a registered trademark of Disney/Pixar.

Index

Selected Bibliography

Books & Other Publications

- *Lizards in Captivity,* Richard H. Wynne, TFH Publications, Neptune, NJ, 1990.
- *Lizards of the World,* Chris Mattison, Blandford, London, England, 1998.
- *Handbook of Lizards,* Hobart M. Smith, Comstock Publishing/Cornell, Ithaca, NY, 1995.
- *The Life of Reptiles,* Angus d'ABellairs, Universe Books, New York, NY, 1970.
- *Lizards, Vol. 2,* Manfred Rogner, Krieger Publishing, Melbourne, FL, 1997.
- *Anoles,* W.P. Mara, Capstone Press, Mankato, MN, 1996.
- *Florida's Fabulous Reptiles & Amphibians,* Peter Carmichael et al., World Publications, Santa Barbara, CA, 1991.
- *Herpetology: Introductory Biology of Amphibians & Reptiles,* 2nd Ed., George Zug, Academic Press U.S., San Diego, CA, 2001.
- *Lizards,* David R. Moenich, TFH Publications, Neptune, NJ, 1990.
- *Green Anoles: General Care & Maintenance,* Phillipe de Vosjol, Advanced Vivarium Systems, Mission Viejo, CA, 1992.
- *Green Anoles: Selection, Care & Breeding,* Ray Hunziker, TFH Publications, Neptune, NJ, 1994.
- *The Iguanid Lizards of Cuba,* Lourdes Rodriguez-Schettino, Univ. Press of Florida, Gainesville, FL, 1999.
- *Caribbean Anoles,* Ralf Heselhaus et al., TFH Publications, Neptune, NJ, 1996.
- *Institute for Laboratory Animal Research (ILAR) Journal,* Vol. 45, #1, "The Green Anole (Anolis Carolinensis): A Reptilian Model for Lab Studies," Matthew B. Lovern et al., 2004.

Web Sites

Green Anole Facts, Dr. Thomas Jenssen:
  www.biology.vt.edu/faculty/jenssen
Brown Anole Invader Species, Dr. Todd Campbell:
  http://invasions.bio.utk.edu/invaders/sagrei.html
Anole Care ("Under the Leaves"): *www.kingsnake.com/anolecare*
Gecko Feet Adhesion, Dr. Kellar Autumn: *www.lclark.edu/~autumn/dept*
Florida Native Plant Society: *www.fnps.org*

CC Clearly, the green anole is not just another dime-store disposable pet. For many of us, the green anole gave us our first encounter with reptiles. More often than not, our ignorance about its needs and habits has been to the anole's detriment. Ultimately, the slender beauty and curious social behavior of the green anole are best observed under natural conditions. JJ

—*Professor Thomas A. Jenssen, Virginia Tech University, Blacksburg, VA*

Who Wrote This Book?

Steven B. "Steve" Isham resides in Orlando and has lived in Florida for over 35 years. A graduate of the University of Central Florida with a BA degree in communications/journalism, he has held a variety of professional writing and marketing positions. Interests include photography, guitar, the outdoors, and travel. This book, his first, is the product of personal observations, research, and interviews with specialists who work with anoles and other reptiles.

Need a Copy of This Book?

Look for *Anoles: Those Florida Yard Lizards* at your local bookstore. However, if you are having trouble finding a copy for sale in your area, please contact us directly on the worldwide web at:

www.anolebook.com

Or write to:
Publisher
Commahawk Publishing, LLC
PO Box 547873
Orlando, FL 32854-7873

Quantity Discounts

Do you need multiple copies of this book for your organization? If so, please ask us about quantity discounts!